EVOLVE

STUDENT'S BOOK

Leslie Anne Hendra, Mark Ibbotson,
and Kathryn O'Dell

3B

CAMBRIDGE
UNIVERSITY PRESS

CAMBRIDGE
UNIVERSITY PRESS

University Printing House, Cambridge CB2 8BS, United Kingdom

One Liberty Plaza, 20th Floor, New York, NY 10006, USA

477 Williamstown Road, Port Melbourne, VIC 3207, Australia

314–321, 3rd Floor, Plot 3, Splendor Forum, Jasola District Centre, New Delhi – 110025, India

79 Anson Road, #06–04/06, Singapore 079906

Cambridge University Press is part of the University of Cambridge.

It furthers the University's mission by disseminating knowledge in the pursuit of education, learning, and research at the highest international levels of excellence.

www.cambridge.org
Information on this title: www.cambridge.org/9781108409209

First published 2019

20 19 18 17 16 15 14 13 12 11 10 9 8 7 6 5 4 3 2 1

Printed in Dubai by Oriental Press

A catalogue record for this publication is available from the British Library

ISBN 978-1-108-40527-0 Student's Book
ISBN 978-1-108-40507-2 Student's Book A
ISBN 978-1-108-40920-9 Student's Book B
ISBN 978-1-108-40528-7 Student's Book with Practice Extra
ISBN 978-1-108-40508-9 Student's Book with Practice Extra A
ISBN 978-1-108-40921-6 Student's Book with Practice Extra B
ISBN 978-1-108-40900-1 Workbook with Audio
ISBN 978-1-108-40872-1 Workbook with Audio A
ISBN 978-1-108-41193-6 Workbook with Audio B
ISBN 978-1-108-40517-1 Teacher's Edition with Test Generator
ISBN 978-1-108-41068-7 Presentation Plus
ISBN 978-1-108-41203-2 Class Audio CDs
ISBN 978-1-108-40793-9 Video Resource Book with DVD
ISBN 978-1-108-41447-0 Full Contact with DVD
ISBN 978-1-108-41154-7 Full Contact A with DVD
ISBN 978-1-108-41415-9 Full Contact B with DVD

Additional resources for this publication at www.cambridge.org/evolve

ACKNOWLEDGMENTS

To our student contributors, who have given us their ideas and their time, and who appear throughout this book:

Angie Melissa González Chaverra, Colombia; Andres Ramírez, Mexico; Celeste María Erazo Flores, Honduras; Brenda Tabora Melgar, Honduras; Andrea Vásquez Mota, Mexico.

Author

The authors and publishers acknowledge the following sources of copyright material and are grateful for the permissions granted. While every effort has been made, it has not always been possible to identify the sources of all the material used, or to trace all copyright holders. If any omissions are brought to our notice, we will be happy to include the appropriate acknowledgements on reprinting and in the next update to the digital edition, as applicable.

Photographs

Key: BG = Background, BC = Below Centre, BL = Below Left, BR = Below Right, CL= Centre Left, CR = Centre Right, TL = Top Left, TR = Top Right.

The following photographs are sourced from Getty Images.

p. xvi: Peter Muller/Cultura; p. xvi, p. 82 (TR): Hill Street Studios/Blend Images; p. 82 (list): Steve Debenport/E+; p. 82 (TC): JGI/Jamie Grill/Blend Images; p. 122: monkeybusinessimages/iStock/Getty Images Plus; 74, 84, 94, 106, 116, 126: Tom Merton/Caiaimage; p. 126 (TR): vgajic/E+; p. 76 (Min-hee): Inti St Clair/Blend Images; p.68: Robert Daly/Caiaimage; p. 72, p. 84 (hiking), p. 90 (TR), p. 102 (woman): Hero Images; p. 65, p. 88: PeopleImages/DigitalVision; p. 66: Fuse/Corbis; p. 67: John Shearer/TAS18/Getty Images Entertainment; p. 69: fredmantel/iStock/Getty Images Plus; p. 70: Caiaimage/Sam Edwards; p. 71: lisegagne/E+; p. 73: ajr_images/iStock/Getty Images Plus; p. 74 (TL): JohnGollop/E+; p. 74 (TR): Coprid/iStock/Getty Images Plus; p. 74 (CL): DrPAS/iStock/Getty Images Plus; p. 74 (CR): PetlinDmitry/iStock/Getty Images Plus; p. 75: Elizabethsalleebauer/RooM; p. 76 (Vanessa): Yuri_Arcurs/iStock/Getty Images Plus; p. 76 (Rodney): xavierarnau/iStock/Getty Images Plus; p. 77: MOHAMMED ABED/AFP; p. 78: lovro77/E+; p. 79: eclipse_images/E+; p. 80: fstop123/iStock/Getty Images Plus; p. 81: Tempura/E+; p. 82 (TL): Rawpixel/iStock/Getty Images Plus; p. 83: Sidekick/E+; p. 84 (reading): Jupiterimages/Creatas/Getty Images Plus; p. 84 (gym): LUNAMARINA/iStock/Getty Images Plus; p. 84 (kitchen): antonio arcos aka fotonstudio photography/Moment; p. 84 (picnic), p. 118: Mint Images; p. 84 (planning): skynesher/E+; p. 85: Simon Ritzmann/The Image Bank; p. 86: TommasoT/E+; p. 87: Andrew Smith/EyeEm; p. 89: Joos Mind/Stone; p. 90 (TL): miljko/E+; p. 90 (BR): hxdyl/iStock/Getty Images Plus; p. 91: Thomas Barwick/DigitalVision; p. 94: kupicoo/E+; p. 96: Paul; p. 97: White Packert/The Image Bank; p. 98: Alexander Spatari/Moment; p. 99 (cotton): SM Rafiq Photography./Moment; p. 99 (glass): Buena Vista Images/DigitalVision; p. 99 (plastic): Thanatham Piriyakarnjanakul/EyeEm; p. 99 (wood): Yevgen Romanenko/Moment; p. 100: Wavebreakmedia/iStock/Getty Images Plus; p. 101: AleksandarGeorgiev/E+; p. 102 (TL): John_Kasawa/iStock/Getty Images Plus; p. 102 (TC): AnikaSalsera/iStock/Getty Images Plus; p. 102 (TR): fcafotodigital/E+; p. 103: Mark de Leeuw; p. 104 (TL): fcafotodigital/iStock/Getty Images Plus; p. 104 (TR): Siphotography/iStock/Getty Images Plus; p. 105: Richard Newstead/Moment; p. 107: Henn Photography/Cultura; p. 108: Brad Barket/Getty Images Entertainment; p. 109: Klaus Vedfelt/DigitalVision; p. 110: Douglas Sacha/Moment; p. 111: Christoph Jorda/Corbis; p. 112: altrendo images/Juice Images; p. 113 (CR): Philippe TURPIN/Photononstop; p. 114: Markus Gann/EyeEm; p. 115 (TR): Irin Na-Ui/EyeEm; p. 115 (TL): Emiliano Granado; p. 116 (Indra Nooyi): Monica Schipper/Getty Images Entertainment; p. 116 (Lin-Manuel): Dia Dipasupil/Getty Images Entertainment; p. 116 (Angela Merkel): Xander Heinl/Photothek; p. 116 (Neil): Ilya S. Savenok/Getty Images Entertainment; 116 (Misty): Vincent Sandoval/Getty Images Entertainment; p. 117: sturti/E+; p. 119: sawaddee3002/iStock/Getty Images Plus; p. 120: JodiJacobson/E+; p. 121: Trevor Williams/Taxi Japan; p. 123: Adie Bush/Cultura; p. 124 (TL): Nick David/Taxi; p. 124 (TR): PJB/Photodisc; p. 125: Brand X Pictures/DigitalVision; p. 126 (TL): Ascent Xmedia/Stone; p. 126 (CL): Paul Bradbury/OJO Images; p. 126 (CR): Peter Cade/The Image Bank; p. 128: Thomas Northcut/DigitalVision; p. 158: Neustockimages/E+; p. 160: Jon Feingersh/Blend Images.

Front cover photography by Orbon Alija/E+.

Illustrations by Gergely Forizs (Beehive illustration) p. 72; Ana Djordjevic (Astound US) p. 106.

Audio production by CityVox, New York.

EVOLVE

SPEAKING MATTERS

EVOLVE is a six-level American English course for adults and young adults, taking students from beginner to advanced levels (CEFR A1 to C1).

Drawing on insights from language teaching experts and real students, EVOLVE is a general English course that gets students speaking with confidence.

This student-centered course covers all skills and focuses on the most effective and efficient ways to make progress in English.

Confidence in teaching.
Joy in learning.

Better Learning WITH EVOLVE

Better Learning is our simple approach where insights we've gained from research have helped shape content that drives results. Language evolves, and so does the way we learn. This course takes a flexible, student-centered approach to English language teaching.

Meet our student contributors

Videos and ideas from real students feature throughout the Student's Book.

Our student contributors describe themselves in three words.

ANDRES RAMÍREZ
Friendly, happy, funny
Instituto Tecnológico de Morelia, México

BRENDA TABORA MELGAR
Honest, easygoing, funny
Centro Universitario Tecnológico, Honduras

ANGIE MELISSA GONZÁLEZ CHAVERRA
Intelligent, creative, passionate
Centro Colombo Americano, Colombia

ANDREA VÁSQUEZ MOTA
Creative, fun, nice
The Institute, Boca del Rio, México

CELESTE MARÍA ERAZO FLORES
Happy, special, friendly
Unitec (Universidad Tecnológica Centroamericana), Honduras

Student-generated content

EVOLVE is the first course of its kind to feature real student-generated content. We spoke to over 2,000 students from all over the world about the topics they would like to discuss in English and in what situations they would like to be able to speak more confidently.

The ideas are included throughout the Student's Book and the students appear in short videos responding to discussion questions.

INSIGHT

Research shows that achievable speaking role models can be a powerful motivator.

CONTENT

Bite-sized videos feature students talking about topics in the Student's Book.

RESULT

Students are motivated to speak and share their ideas.

"It's important to provide learners with interesting or stimulating topics."

Teacher, Mexico (Global Teacher Survey, 2017)

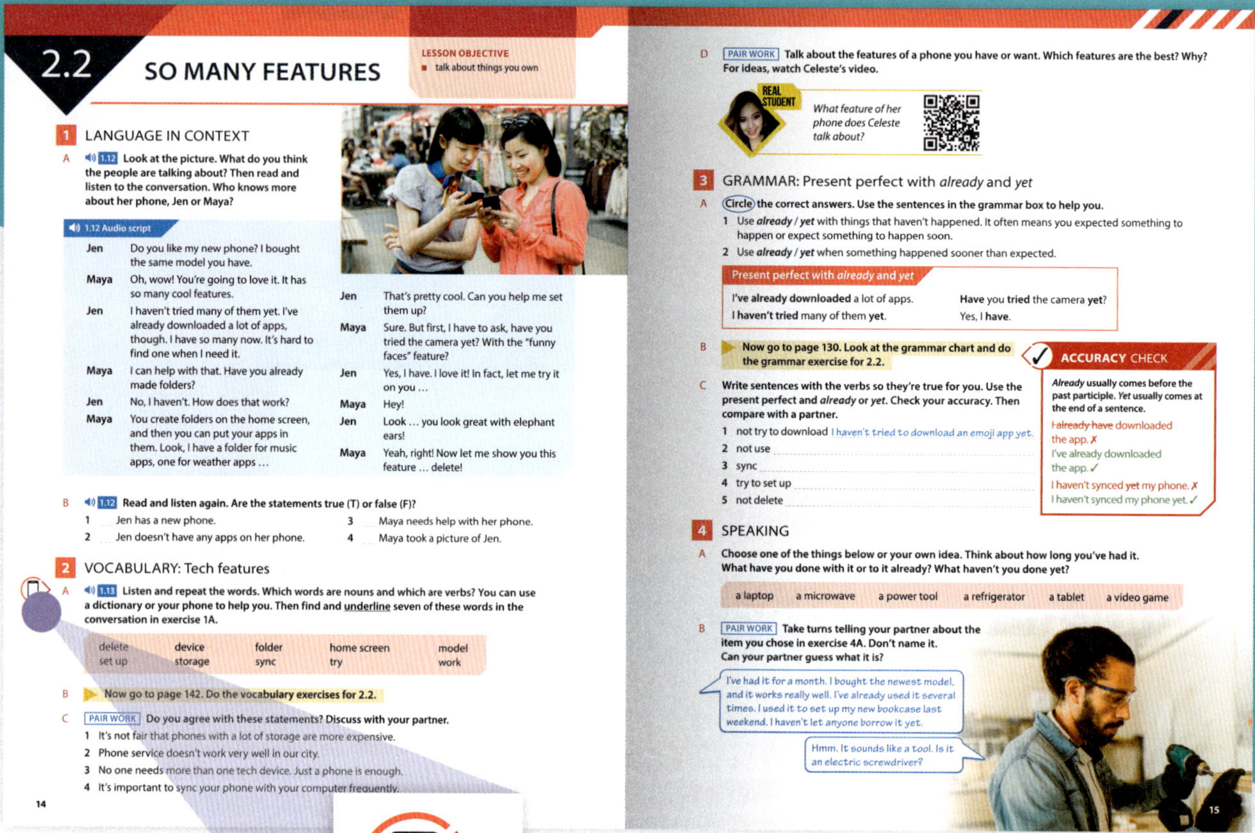

2.2 SO MANY FEATURES

LESSON OBJECTIVE
- talk about things you own

1 LANGUAGE IN CONTEXT

A 1.12 Look at the picture. What do you think the people are talking about? Then read and listen to the conversation. Who knows more about her phone, Jen or Maya?

1.12 Audio script

Jen	Do you like my new phone? I bought the same model you have.
Maya	Oh, wow! You're going to love it. It has so many cool features.
Jen	I haven't tried many of them yet. I've already downloaded a lot of apps, though. I have so many now. It's hard to find one when I need it.
Maya	I can help with that. Have you already made folders?
Jen	No, I haven't. How does that work?
Maya	You create folders on the home screen, and then you can put your apps in them. Look, I have a folder for music apps, one for weather apps …
Jen	That's pretty cool. Can you help me set them up?
Maya	Sure. But first, I have to ask, have you tried the camera yet? With the "funny faces" feature?
Jen	Yes, I have. I love it! In fact, let me try it on you …
Maya	Hey!
Jen	Look … you look great with elephant ears!
Maya	Yeah, right! Now let me show you this feature … delete!

B 1.12 Read and listen again. Are the statements true (T) or false (F)?

1 Jen has a new phone.
2 Jen doesn't have any apps on her phone.
3 Maya needs help with her phone.
4 Maya took a picture of Jen.

2 VOCABULARY: Tech features

A 1.13 Listen and repeat the words. Which words are nouns and which are verbs? You can use a dictionary or your phone to help you. Then find and underline seven of these words in the conversation in exercise 1A.

delete, set up, device, storage, folder, sync, home screen, try, model, work

B Now go to page 142. Do the vocabulary exercises for 2.2.

C PAIR WORK Do you agree with these statements? Discuss with your partner.

1 It's not fair that phones with a lot of storage are more expensive.
2 Phone service doesn't work very well in our city.
3 No one needs more than one tech device. Just a phone is enough.
4 It's important to sync your phone with your computer frequently.

14

D PAIR WORK Talk about the features of a phone you have or want. Which features are the best? Why? For ideas, watch Celeste's video.

REAL STUDENT
What feature of her phone does Celeste talk about?

3 GRAMMAR: Present perfect with *already* and *yet*

A Circle the correct answers. Use the sentences in the grammar box to help you.

1 Use *already* / *yet* with things that haven't happened. It often means you expected something to happen or expect something to happen soon.
2 Use *already* / *yet* when something happened sooner than expected.

Present perfect with *already* and *yet*

I've already downloaded a lot of apps. / Have you tried the camera yet?
I haven't tried many of them yet. / Yes, I have.

B Now go to page 130. Look at the grammar chart and do the grammar exercise for 2.2.

C Write sentences with the verbs so they're true for you. Use the present perfect and *already* or *yet*. Check your accuracy. Then compare with a partner.

1 not try to download *I haven't tried to download an emoji app yet.*
2 not use
3 sync
4 try to set up
5 not delete

ACCURACY CHECK

Already usually comes before the past participle. *Yet* usually comes at the end of a sentence.

~~I already have~~ downloaded the app. ✗
I've already downloaded the app. ✓
I haven't synced yet my phone. ✗
I haven't synced my phone yet. ✓

4 SPEAKING

A Choose one of the things below or your own idea. Think about how long you've had it. What have you done with it or to it already? What haven't you done yet?

a laptop, a microwave, a power tool, a refrigerator, a tablet, a video game

B PAIR WORK Take turns telling your partner about the item you chose in exercise 4A. Don't name it. Can your partner guess what it is?

I've had it for a month. I bought the newest model, and it works really well. I've already used it several times. I used it to set up my new bookcase last weekend. I haven't let anyone borrow it yet.

Hmm. It sounds like a tool. Is it an electric screwdriver?

15

Find it

INSIGHT

Research with hundreds of teachers and students across the globe revealed a desire to expand the classroom and bring the real world in.

CONTENT

Find it are smartphone activities that allow students to bring live content into the class and personalize the learning experience with research and group activities.

RESULT

Students engage in the lesson because it is meaningful to them.

Designed for success

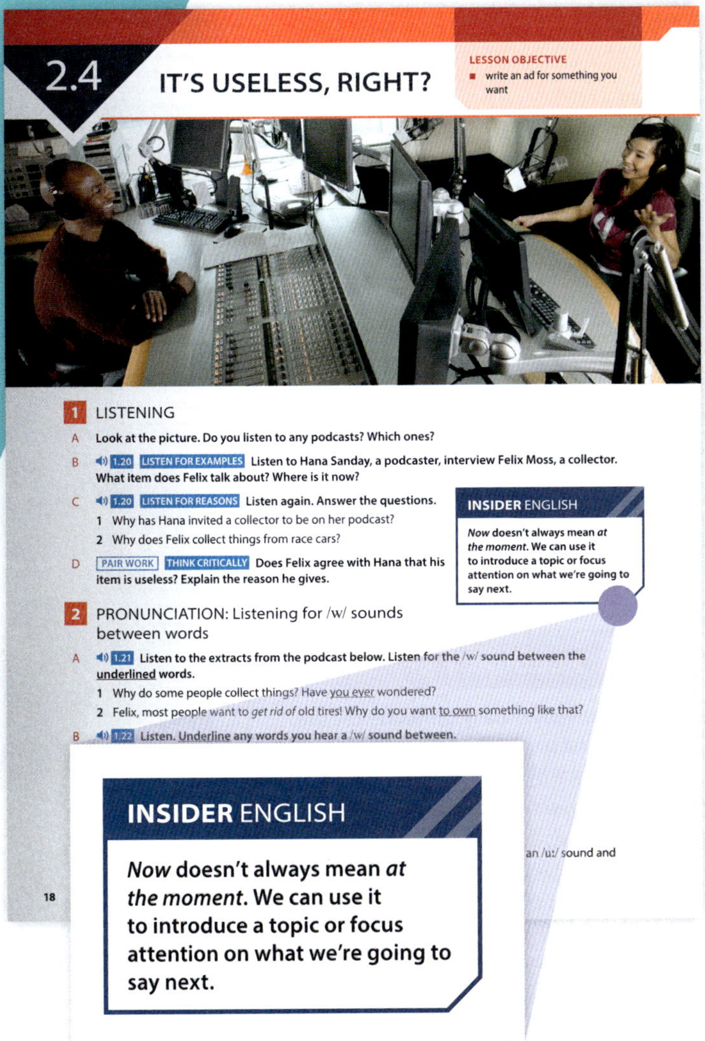
2.4 IT'S USELESS, RIGHT?

LESSON OBJECTIVE
- write an ad for something you want

1 LISTENING

A Look at the picture. Do you listen to any podcasts? Which ones?

B 1.20 LISTEN FOR EXAMPLES Listen to Hana Sanday, a podcaster, interview Felix Moss, a collector. What item does Felix talk about? Where is it now?

C 1.20 LISTEN FOR REASONS Listen again. Answer the questions.
1 Why has Hana invited a collector to be on her podcast?
2 Why does Felix collect things from race cars?

D PAIR WORK THINK CRITICALLY Does Felix agree with Hana that his item is useless? Explain the reason he gives.

INSIDER ENGLISH

Now doesn't always mean *at the moment*. We can use it to introduce a topic or focus attention on what we're going to say next.

2 PRONUNCIATION: Listening for /w/ sounds between words

A 1.21 Listen to the extracts from the podcast below. Listen for the /w/ sound between the underlined words.
1 Why do some people collect things? Have you ever wondered?
2 Felix, most people want to *get rid of* old tires! Why do you want to own something like that?

B 1.22 Listen. Underline any words you hear a /w/ sound between.

an /uː/ sound and

18

INSIDER ENGLISH

Now doesn't always mean *at the moment*. We can use it to introduce a topic or focus attention on what we're going to say next.

Pronunciation

INSIGHT

Research shows that only certain aspects of pronunciation actually affect comprehensibility and inhibit communication.

CONTENT

EVOLVE focuses on the aspects of pronunciation that most affect communication.

RESULT

Students understand more when listening and can be clearly understood when they speak.

Insider English

INSIGHT

Even in a short exchange, idiomatic language can inhibit understanding.

CONTENT

Insider English focuses on the informal language and colloquial expressions frequently found in everyday situations.

RESULT

Students are confident in the real world.

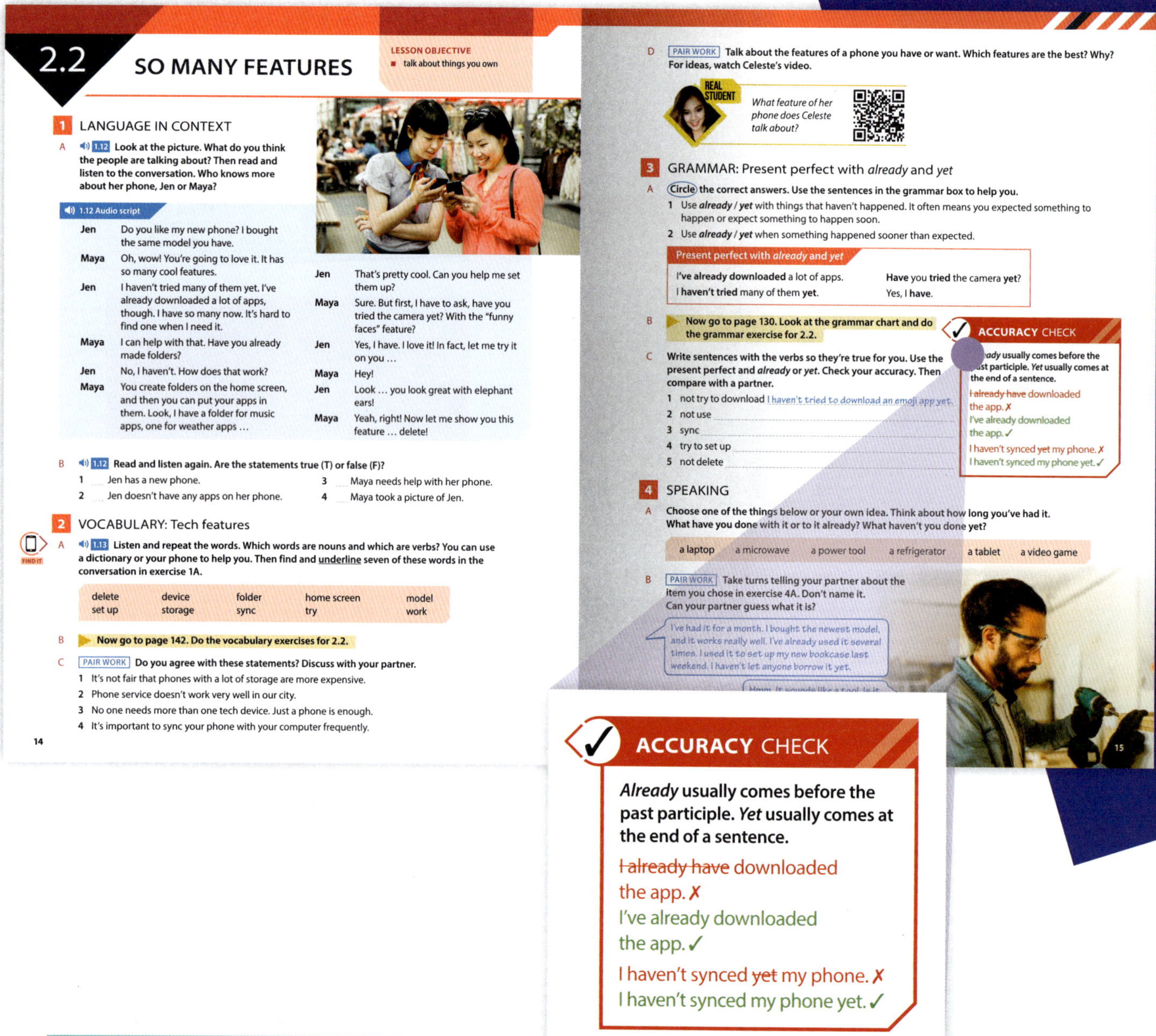

2.2 SO MANY FEATURES

LESSON OBJECTIVE
- talk about things you own

1 LANGUAGE IN CONTEXT

A 1.12 Look at the picture. What do you think the people are talking about? Then read and listen to the conversation. Who knows more about her phone, Jen or Maya?

1.12 Audio script

Jen Do you like my new phone? I bought the same model you have.
Maya Oh, wow! You're going to love it. It has so many cool features.
Jen I haven't tried many of them yet. I've already downloaded a lot of apps, though. I have so many now. It's hard to find one when I need it.
Maya I can help with that. Have you already made folders?
Jen No, I haven't. How does that work?
Maya You create folders on the home screen, and then you can put your apps in them. Look, I have a folder for music apps, one for weather apps …
Jen That's pretty cool. Can you help me set them up?
Maya Sure. But first, I have to ask, have you tried the camera yet? With the "funny faces" feature?
Jen Yes, I have. I love it! In fact, let me try it on you …
Maya Hey!
Jen Look … you look great with elephant ears!
Maya Yeah, right! Now let me show you this feature … delete!

B 1.12 Read and listen again. Are the statements true (T) or false (F)?
1 ___ Jen has a new phone.
2 ___ Jen doesn't have any apps on her phone.
3 ___ Maya needs help with her phone.
4 ___ Maya took a picture of Jen.

2 VOCABULARY: Tech features

FIND IT

A 1.13 Listen and repeat the words. Which words are nouns and which are verbs? You can use a dictionary or your phone to help you. Then find and underline seven of these words in the conversation in exercise 1A.

delete device folder home screen model
set up storage sync try work

B Now go to page 142. Do the vocabulary exercises for 2.2.

C PAIR WORK Do you agree with these statements? Discuss with your partner.
1 It's not fair that phones with a lot of storage are more expensive.
2 Phone service doesn't work very well in our city.
3 No one needs more than one tech device. Just a phone is enough.
4 It's important to sync your phone with your computer frequently.

14

D PAIR WORK Talk about the features of a phone you have or want. Which features are the best? Why? For ideas, watch Celeste's video.

REAL STUDENT
What feature of her phone does Celeste talk about?

3 GRAMMAR: Present perfect with *already* and *yet*

A Circle the correct answers. Use the sentences in the grammar box to help you.
1 Use *already* / *yet* with things that haven't happened. It often means you expected something to happen or expect something to happen soon.
2 Use *already* / *yet* when something happened sooner than expected.

Present perfect with *already* and *yet*

I've already downloaded a lot of apps.	Have you tried the camera yet?
I haven't tried many of them yet.	Yes, I have.

B Now go to page 130. Look at the grammar chart and do the grammar exercise for 2.2.

C Write sentences with the verbs so they're true for you. Use the present perfect and *already* or *yet*. Check your accuracy. Then compare with a partner.
1 not try to download I haven't tried to download an emoji app yet.
2 not use
3 sync
4 try to set up
5 not delete

4 SPEAKING

A Choose one of the things below or your own idea. Think about how long you've had it. What have you done with it or to it already? What haven't you done yet?

a laptop a microwave a power tool a refrigerator a tablet a video game

B PAIR WORK Take turns telling your partner about the item you chose in exercise 4A. Don't name it. Can your partner guess what it is?

I've had it for a month. I bought the newest model, and it works really well. I've already used it several times. I used it to set up my new bookcase last weekend. I haven't let anyone borrow it yet.

15

ACCURACY CHECK

Already usually comes before the past participle. *Yet* usually comes at the end of a sentence.

~~I already have~~ downloaded the app. ✗
I've already downloaded the app. ✓
I haven't synced ~~yet~~ my phone. ✗
I haven't synced my phone yet. ✓

Accuracy check

INSIGHT

Some common errors can become fossilized if not addressed early on in the learning process.

CONTENT

Accuracy check highlights common learner errors (based on unique research into the Cambridge Learner Corpus) and can be used for self-editing.

RESULT

Students avoid common errors in their written and spoken English.

“The presentation is very clear and there are plenty of opportunities for student practice and production.”

Jason Williams, Teacher, Notre Dame Seishin University, Japan

2.4 IT'S USELESS, RIGHT?

LESSON OBJECTIVE
- write an ad for something you want

1 LISTENING

A Look at the picture. Do you listen to any podcasts? Which ones?

B 1.20 LISTEN FOR EXAMPLES Listen to Hana Sanday, a podcaster, interview Felix Moss, a collector. What item does Felix talk about? Where is it now?

C 1.20 LISTEN FOR REASONS Listen again. Answer the questions.
1 Why has Hana invited a collector to be on her podcast?
2 Why does Felix collect things from race cars?

D PAIR WORK THINK CRITICALLY Does Felix agree with Hana that his item is useless? Explain the reason he gives.

INSIDER ENGLISH
Now doesn't always mean *at the moment*. We can use it to introduce a topic or focus attention on what we're going to say next.

2 PRONUNCIATION: Listening for /w/ sounds between words

A 1.21 Listen to the extracts from the podcast below. Listen for the /w/ sound between the underlined words.
1 Why do some people collect things? Have you ever wondered?
2 Felix, most people want to *get rid of* old tires! Why do you want to own something like that?

B 1.22 Listen. Underline any words you hear a /w/ sound between.
A Do you and your brother like to collect things?
B He does. But I do everything I can to avoid collecting useless stuff.
A So do you ever keep things just to keep them?
B I guess I might keep a few if they're things I really like.

C Circle the correct words to complete the statement.
A /w/ sound is often used to connect two words when the first word *starts* / *ends* in an /uː/ sound and the second word starts with a *consonant* / *vowel*.

18

3 WRITING

A Read the online ad. What items does Emilia want? Why does she want them? What kind of personality do you think she has?

Account Ads Messages Post an ad
I'm looking for ... Search

WANTED:
TRAFFIC LIGHT, 2 STOP SIGNS

I'm interested in buying a Canadian traffic light (see picture for an example). Do you have one like this? Or do you know where I can get one? Yes, I know they're on every street corner – but please don't steal one! But seriously, I want one that's legal and that works. I've checked online every day for weeks, but I haven't seen any for sale yet.

I'm also looking for two red stop signs (see picture). They can be old, but they have to be in good condition. I've seen some for sale online, but they were fake, not real ones. I want "the real thing."

You're probably wondering why I want these things. They're for a party, and after that, I'll give them to my niece. She loves stuff like this.

I'll pay a reasonable price for items in good condition. Send an email with photos, and hopefully I can give you a "green light" for a sale. Contact Emilia at:

show contact info

STOP STOP

GLOSSARY
legal (*adj*) allowed by the law

B WRITING SKILLS Read the explanation about using *one* and *ones*. Then find and underline more examples in the ad. What do they refer to?

We use *one* (singular) and *ones* (plural) to avoid repeating a subject we've already mentioned. We use *one* and *ones* when it's clear what they refer to. In the question below, *one* = a Canadian traffic light:

...ght (*see picture for an example*).

REGISTER CHECK
In an ad title, you can leave out unimportant words.
WANTED: TRAFFIC LIGHT, 2 STOP SIGNS =
I want a traffic light and two stop signs.

...u want that is hard to find. Write a short title. Describe the ...e a reason why you want it. You can include pictures. You can ... item.

19

REGISTER CHECK

In an ad title, you can leave out unimportant words.

WANTED: TRAFFIC LIGHT, 2 STOP SIGNS =
I want a traffic light and two stop signs.

Register check

INSIGHT

Teachers report that their students often struggle to master the differences between written and spoken English.

CONTENT

Register check draws on research into the Cambridge English Corpus and highlights potential problem areas for learners.

RESULT

Students transition confidently between written and spoken English and recognize different levels of formality as well as when to use them appropriately.

You spoke. We listened.

Students told us that speaking is the most important skill for them to master, while teachers told us that finding speaking activities which engage their students and work in the classroom can be challenging.

That's why EVOLVE has a whole lesson dedicated to speaking: Lesson 5, *Time to speak*.

Time to speak

INSIGHT

Speaking ability is how students most commonly measure their own progress, but is also the area where they feel most insecure. To be able to fully exploit speaking opportunities in the classroom, students need a safe speaking environment where they can feel confident, supported, and able to experiment with language.

CONTENT

Time to Speak is a unique lesson dedicated to developing speaking skills and is based around immersive tasks which involve information sharing and decision making.

RESULT

Time to speak lessons create a buzz in the classroom where speaking can really thrive, evolve, and take off, resulting in more confident speakers of English.

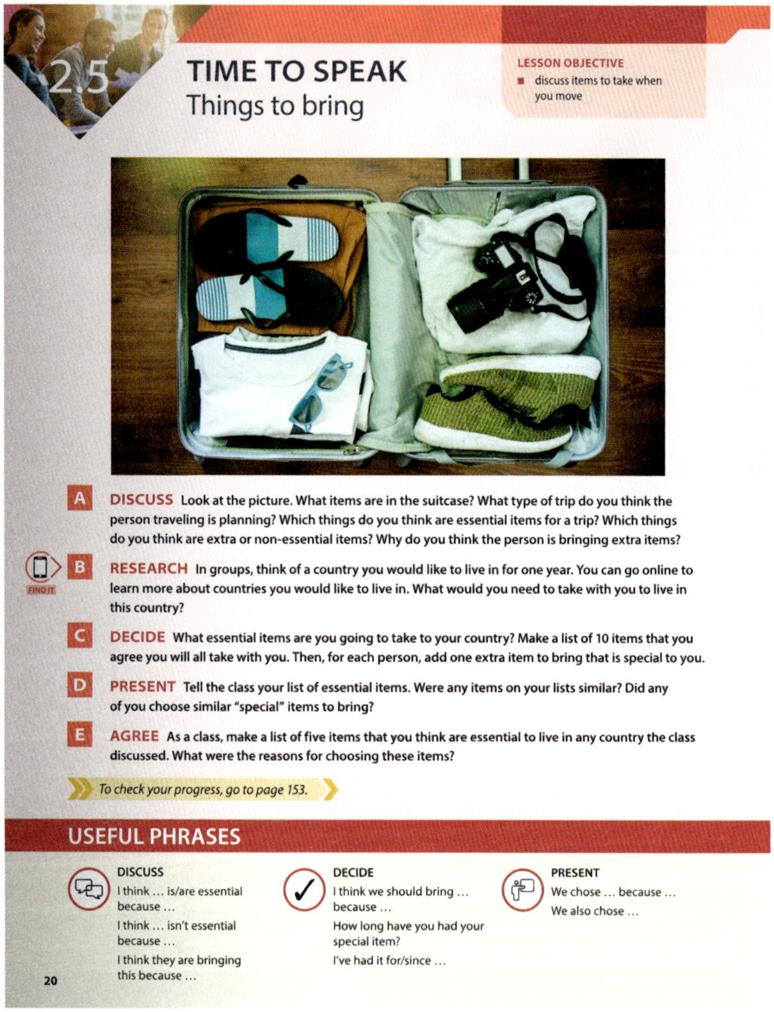

2.5 TIME TO SPEAK
Things to bring

LESSON OBJECTIVE
- discuss items to take when you move

A **DISCUSS** Look at the picture. What items are in the suitcase? What type of trip do you think the person traveling is planning? Which things do you think are essential items for a trip? Which things do you think are extra or non-essential items? Why do you think the person is bringing extra items?

B **RESEARCH** In groups, think of a country you would like to live in for one year. You can go online to learn more about countries you would like to live in. What would you need to take with you to live in this country?

C **DECIDE** What essential items are you going to take to your country? Make a list of 10 items that you agree you will all take with you. Then, for each person, add one extra item to bring that is special to you.

D **PRESENT** Tell the class your list of essential items. Were any items on your lists similar? Did any of you choose similar "special" items to bring?

E **AGREE** As a class, make a list of five items that you think are essential to live in any country the class discussed. What were the reasons for choosing these items?

To check your progress, go to page 153.

USEFUL PHRASES

DISCUSS
I think … is/are essential because …
I think … isn't essential because …
I think they are bringing this because …

DECIDE
I think we should bring … because …
How long have you had your special item?
I've had it for/since …

PRESENT
We chose … because …
We also chose …

20

Experience Better Learning with EVOLVE: a course that helps both teachers and students on every step of the language learning journey.

Speaking matters. Find out more about creating safe speaking environments in the classroom.

EVOLVE unit structure

Unit opening page

Each unit opening page activates prior knowledge and vocabulary and immediately gets students speaking.

Lessons 1 and 2

These lessons present and practice the unit vocabulary and grammar in context, helping students discover language rules for themselves. Students then have the opportunity to use this language in well-scaffolded, personalized speaking tasks.

Lesson 3

This lesson is built around a functional language dialogue that models and contextualizes useful fixed expressions for managing a particular situation. This is a real world strategy to help students handle unexpected conversational turns.

Lesson 4

This is a combined skills lesson based around an engaging reading or listening text. Each lesson asks students to think critically and ends with a practical writing task.

Lesson 5

Time to speak is an entire lesson dedicated to developing speaking skills. Students work on collaborative, immersive tasks which involve information sharing and decision making.

	Learning objectives	Grammar	Vocabulary	Pronunciation
Unit 7 Entertain us	■ Discuss your changing tastes in music ■ Talk about TV shows and movies ■ Refuse invitations and respond to refusals ■ Write a movie review ■ Talk about changing tastes	■ *used to* ■ Comparisons with *(not) as … as*	■ Music ■ TV shows and movies	■ Saying /m/ in *I'm*
Unit 8 Getting there	■ Talk about what you've been doing ■ Talk about progress ■ Catch up with people's news ■ Write a post about managing your time ■ Decide on better ways to use your time	■ Present perfect continuous ■ Present perfect vs. present perfect continuous	■ Describing experiences ■ Describing progress	■ Saying /ɑ/ and /æ/ vowel sounds ■ Listening for weak forms of *didn't*
Unit 9 Make it work	■ Talk about college subjects ■ Discuss rules for working and studying at home ■ Express confidence and lack of confidence ■ Write the main part of a résumé ■ Decide how to use your skills	■ Modals of necessity ■ Modals of prohibition and permission	■ College subjects ■ Employment	■ Grouping words
	Review 3 (Review of Units 7–9)			
Unit 10 Why we buy	■ Say what things are made of ■ Talk about where things come from ■ Question or approve of someone's choices ■ Write feedback about company products ■ Design a commercial	■ Simple present passive ■ Simple past passive	■ Describing materials ■ Production and distribution	■ Saying /u/, /aʊ/, and /ʊ/ vowel sounds ■ Listening for contrastive stress
Unit 11 Pushing yourself	■ Talk about how to succeed ■ Talk about imaginary situations ■ Give opinions and ask for agreement ■ Write a personal story ■ Talk about a person you admire	■ Phrasal verbs ■ Present and future unreal conditionals	■ Succeeding ■ Opportunities and risks	■ Saying /ʃ/ and /ʤ/ sounds
Unit 12 Life's little lessons	■ Talk about accidents ■ Talk about extreme experiences ■ Describe and ask about feelings ■ Write an anecdote about a life lesson ■ Plan a fun learning experience	■ Indefinite pronouns ■ Reported speech	■ Describing accidents ■ Describing extremes	■ Saying *-ed* at the end of a word ■ Listening for *'ll*
	Review 4 (Review of Units 10–12)			
	Grammar charts and practice, pages 135–140	**Vocabulary exercises, pages 147–152**		

Functional language	Listening	Reading	Writing	Speaking
■ Refuse invitations; respond to a refusal **Real-world strategy** ■ Soften comments		**Animation for all ages** ■ An online article about animated movies and TV shows	**A review of an animated movie** ■ A movie review ■ Organizing ideas	■ Talk about how musical tastes have changed ■ Compare favorite movies/ TV shows ■ Invite someone to an event and refuse an invitation ■ Talk about humor in animated movies **Time to speak** ■ Discuss changing tastes in entertainment
■ Say how long it's been; ask about someone's news; answer **Real-world strategy** ■ Use *that would be* to comment on something	**A time-saving tip** ■ A podcast interview about time management		**A post about a podcast** ■ A post about time management ■ Time expressions	■ Talk about what you've been doing recently ■ Explain what you've been spending time on ■ Talk to a friend you haven't seen for a while ■ Talk about someone's new habits **Time to speak** ■ Prioritize tasks to improve balance
■ Express confidence; express lack of confidence **Real-world strategy** ■ Focus on reasons		**A job search** ■ An online job ad and a résumé for the job	**A résumé** ■ Experiences and activities for a résumé ■ How to write a résumé	■ Talk about subjects in school that prepare you for the future ■ Present rules for working or studying at home ■ Discuss plans for doing challenging activities ■ Identify what job an ad is for **Time to speak** ■ Describe skills for an ideal job
■ Question someone's choices; approve someone's choices **Real-world strategy** ■ Change your mind	**Not just customers – fans** ■ A podcast about customers as fans		**Online customer feedback about products** ■ Feedback about products ■ *However* and *although* to contrast ideas	■ Describe how materials affect the environment ■ Share where things you own were produced ■ Talk about things you want to buy ■ Talk about companies you like **Time to speak** ■ Discuss reasons why people buy things
■ Ask for agreement; agree **Real-world strategy** ■ Soften an opinion		**Outside the comfort zone** ■ An online article about benefits of leaving your comfort zone	**A story about a challenging new activity** ■ A story about pushing yourself ■ Comparing facts	■ Talk about a failure and its effects ■ Discuss what you might risk for money ■ Express opinions about topics with two sides ■ Talk about pushing yourself **Time to speak** ■ Discuss what makes people successful
■ Describe your feelings; ask about or guess others' feelings **Real-world strategy** ■ End a story	**Lessons learned?** ■ An expert presentation about life lessons		**A story about learning a lesson** ■ An anecdote about a life lesson ■ Using different expressions with similar meanings	■ Talk about a small, amusing accident ■ Describe an extreme experience ■ Talk about emotions associated with an experience ■ Talk about learning from mistakes **Time to speak** ■ Talk about activities to learn new skills

CLASSROOM LANGUAGE

1.02 PAIR WORK AND GROUP WORK

Choosing roles

Do you want to go first?

I'll be Student A, and you be Student B.

Let's switch roles and do it again.

Eliciting opinions

What do you think, ______ ?

How about you, ______ ?

Asking for clarification or more information

I'm not sure I understand. Can you say that again?

Does anyone have anything to add?

Completing a task

We're done.

We're finished. What should we do now/next?

CHECKING YOUR WORK

Comparing answers

Let's compare answers.

What do you have for number ... ?

I have ...

I have the same thing.

I have something different.

I have a different answer.

Offering feedback

Let's switch papers.

I'm not quite sure what you mean here.

I really like that you ...

It looks like you ...

I wondered about ...

Can you say this another way?

I wanted to ask you about ...

Let's check this one again.

UNIT OBJECTIVES

- discuss your changing tastes in music
- talk about TV shows and movies
- refuse invitations and respond to refusals
- write a movie review
- talk about changing tastes

ENTERTAIN US

7

START SPEAKING

A **What kind of performance is this? How are the people feeling about it?**

B **What makes a performance enjoyable? disappointing? awful?**

C **When did you last go to a concert or another live performance? Describe what it was like. For ideas, watch Brenda's video.**

REAL STUDENT

Did you and Brenda have similar experiences?

7.1 A 50-YEAR PLAYLIST

LESSON OBJECTIVE
- discuss your changing tastes in music

1 VOCABULARY: Music

FIND IT

A 2.02 GROUP WORK **Listen and repeat the words. Name a musician, band, or song for each kind of music. You can go online to learn more about the kinds of music.**

classical	country	EDM	folk	heavy metal
hip-hop	jazz	pop	reggae	rock

B GROUP WORK **Which kinds of music do you like or dislike? Is there one kind of music you all like?**

C **Now go to page 147. Do the vocabulary exercises for 7.1.**

2 LANGUAGE IN CONTEXT

A **Look at the picture of Hugo and his son Logan. They're talking about music. What kind of music do you think each one likes?**

B 2.03 **Read and listen. They are planning the music for Hugo's 50th birthday party. What kinds of music do they mention?**

C 2.03 **Read and listen again. Answer the questions.**

1 How is Hugo planning to choose the songs?
2 Which is bigger, his digital music collection or his CD collection?

2.03 Audio script

Logan So, have you chosen the songs for your playlist yet?

Hugo No, but I've decided to choose music from different stages of my life.

Logan Cool. So, first – your teenage years, I guess. What did you use to listen to then?

Hugo **Pop** and **rock** … and **heavy metal.** I used to listen to a lot of heavy metal. I still listen to it sometimes.

Logan I know. I hear it every time I'm in the car with you! What about **folk**?

Hugo Folk? No way! But I used to like **country** when I was in my 30s.

Logan I've never heard you play country music.

Hugo Yeah. I'm not into it anymore, but I'll put some on my playlist.

Logan What other stuff did you listen to?

Hugo Not much. Actually, I listen to more music now than I used to, thanks to downloading and streaming. I didn't use to buy much music in the past because it was harder to get.

Logan Are you kidding? You have tons of CDs.

Hugo That's nothing. My digital collection is much bigger. Anyway, I don't listen to CDs much anymore. Only the heavy metal ones – in the car – just for you!

D PAIR WORK **Imagine you're planning a playlist for a big family party. Decide what kinds of music to play so there's something for everyone.**

INSIDER ENGLISH

We can use the informal expression *thanks to* + something or someone. It means *because of*.

3 GRAMMAR: *used to*

A Circle the correct answers. Use the sentences in the grammar box to help you.

1 In affirmative sentences, use ***use to*** / ***used to*** and the base form of a verb.

2 In negative sentences, use *didn't* with ***use to*** / ***used to*** and the base form of a verb.

3 In questions, use *did* with ***use to*** / ***used to*** and the base form of a verb.

> ***used to***
>
> What did you **use to listen** to then?
>
> I **used to like** country music.
>
> I **didn't use to buy** much music.

B **Choose the correct answers.**

1 I **used to / didn't use to** like jazz, but I don't like it anymore.

2 I **used to / didn't use to** like EDM, but now I love it.

3 I **used to / didn't use to** listen to a lot of classical music. I still do, sometimes.

4 I **used to / didn't use to** have a lot of country music, but now I don't.

C **Now go to page 135. Look at the grammar chart and do the grammar exercise for 7.1.**

D **Complete the questions with *you*, the correct form of *used to*, and the verbs in parentheses ( ). Check your accuracy. Then ask your partner the questions.**

1 When you were 13, who ______________ (listen) to music with?

2 What kind of concerts ______________ (go) to?

3 Which singers ______________ (like)?

4 Where did you ______________ (buy) music?

5 Did you ______________ (play) an instrument? Which one?

> ✓ **ACCURACY** CHECK
>
> **Be careful not to confuse *usually* and *used to*. Don't use them in the same sentence.**
>
> I usually ~~used to~~ listen to hip-hop. ✗
>
> I usually listen to hip-hop. ✓
> (present habit)
>
> I used to listen to heavy metal. ✓
> (past habit)

4 SPEAKING

A **Think about how your musical tastes have changed. What kind of music did you use to like? Which artists did you use to listen to? What do you listen to now? Who are your favorite artists? Make notes.**

B GROUP WORK **Describe your changing musical tastes. How much do you have in common?**

> I used to love rock music. When I was 13, rock was all I listened to. Now I like pop music. My favorite artist is Camila Cabello.

7.2 THE BEST ENTERTAINMENT

LESSON OBJECTIVE
- talk about TV shows and movies

1 VOCABULARY: TV shows and movies

A 2.04 PAIR WORK **Listen and repeat the words. Which can describe movies? Which can describe TV shows? Which can describe both?**

animated movie	comedy	documentary	drama	game show
horror	musical	reality show	romantic comedy	science fiction
soap opera	talk show	thriller		

B PAIR WORK **Give an example of each kind of movie or show in exercise 1A.**

C **Now go to page 147. Do the vocabulary exercises for 7.2.**

2 LANGUAGE IN CONTEXT

A **Read the article. What do *the small screen* and *the big screen* mean?**

Big screen or small screen?

You sit down after a long day and open an app on your smartphone. What are you going to watch this time? Maybe an episode of your favorite **game show** or **soap opera**? Your roommates are on the couch, using a tablet to binge-watch episodes of a popular **drama** series. Your friend texts you about the **documentary** she's watching on her laptop.

Many viewers think that personal devices are as good as TVs. We watch a lot of movies and TV shows on the "small screen" instead of the "big screen." But is it the same? If you like **science fiction**, you probably love special effects – the way monsters look or the way spaceships fly through the air. But on a phone, the effects aren't as exciting as they are in the theater. Watching a **horror** movie at home isn't as frightening as watching it in a dark theater. (Although maybe that's a good thing!)

Do you like watching shows on your device as much as watching on a big screen? Maybe it depends on the genre. Nothing is as much fun as watching reality shows on one big screen with your friends – and laughing together.

B **Read again. How does the article suggest watching shows and movies in different ways gives people a different experience?**

C **Guess the meaning of these words from context. Match the words (1–5) to the definitions (a–e).**

1 episode ____   a set of television broadcasts using the same characters but in different situations
2 series ____   b a style of TV show or movie
3 binge-watch ____   c people who watch TV or movies
4 viewers ____   d one of the parts of a television or radio program
5 genre ____   e watch a lot of episodes in a short amount of time

D PAIR WORK **Do you like watching TV shows and movies on a small screen or a big screen? Does it matter to you? What are the pros and cons of each option? For ideas, watch Angie's video.**

REAL STUDENT

Do you and Angie agree on how you like to watch TV shows and movies?

3 GRAMMAR: Comparisons with (*not*) *as … as*

A **Circle the correct answers. Use the sentences in the grammar box to help you.**

1 *as … as* means **the same as** / **different from**.

2 *not as … as* means **more than** / **less than**.

> **Comparisons with (*not*) *as … as***
>
> Many viewers think that personal devices are **as good as** TVs.
>
> Nothing is **as much fun as** watching reality shows with your friends.
>
> Watching a horror movie at home is**n't as frightening as** watching it in a dark theater.
>
> Do you like watching on your device **as much as** watching on a big screen?

B **Rewrite the sentences with (*not*) *as … as* so that they mean the same. Then think of a TV series for one or more of the sentences.**

1 The first season is better than the second season.
The second season ___isn't as good as___ the first season.

2 The first season and the second season are both good.
The second season ______________ the first season.

3 The second season has more special effects than the first season.
The first season ______________ the second season.

4 I liked watching the first season more than the second season.
I ______________ the second season ______________ the first season.

C Now go to page 135. Look at the grammar chart and do the grammar exercise for 7.2.

D PAIR WORK **Talk about two movies you've watched that have a similar story or the same characters. Compare them using (*not*) *as … as*. Do you and your partner have the same opinion?**

4 SPEAKING

A **Look at the shows and movies in exercise 1A. Choose your three favorites kinds of shows and movies (for example, documentaries, comedies, and thrillers). For each kind, choose your favorite movie or show.**

B PAIR WORK **Talk about your favorite shows. Why do you think your favorites are the best and the others aren't as good? Do you like the same shows?**

My favorites are science fiction, thrillers, and reality shows. My favorite science fiction movie is …

Oh, I like science fiction, too! But my favorite movie is …

7.3 A NEW BAND

LESSON OBJECTIVE
- refuse invitations and respond to refusals

1 FUNCTIONAL LANGUAGE

A 2.05 **Look at the picture. What do you think is happening? Then read and listen. What does Cody invite Mari to do? Why does Mari say she can't go?**

2.05 Audio script

A Hey, Mari. Did I tell you I'm learning to play the banjo?

B Yeah, actually, you've mentioned it a few times.

A But you haven't seen my new banjo. I have a picture of it on my phone …

B We should drink our coffee before it gets cold. **Maybe after that.**

A OK. Well, anyway, I know I haven't told you this: I started a country band with a few students in my music class.

B A band? That's cool, Cody. Country isn't my favorite, but I bet you guys are great.

A Well, we're not perfect. But we think we'll get better if we play in front of an audience. So, I was wondering, would you like to hear us play? We're having our first concert on Friday night.

B Um, **I'd love to, but** I can't make it on Friday. I have … other plans. **But thanks for asking.**

A **Oh, that's too bad.** Are you free on Saturday?

B **I'm sorry. Unfortunately**, I'm going to be kind of busy all weekend.

A **I understand.** Well, **let me know if your plans change.**

B **Complete the chart with expressions in bold from the conversation above.**

Refusing invitations	Responding to a refusal
Maybe [1] ________ . / Maybe later.	Oh, that's [6] ________ .
I'd [2] ________ , but …	I [7] ________ .
But thanks [3] ________ .	Let me know if [8] ________ .
I'm [4] ________ . [5] ________ , …	Let me know if you change your mind.

C PAIR WORK **Choose the correct response to each sentence. Then practice the conversations with your partner.**

1 **A** Do you want to go to a movie on Friday night?
 B **a** Let me know if your plans change. **b** I'm sorry. Unfortunately, I have to work.

2 **A** I'm sorry I can't go to your soccer game on Saturday.
 B **a** I understand. **b** I'd love to.

3 **A** Do you want to come over for dinner tonight?
 B **a** But thanks for asking. **b** I'd love to, but I already have plans.

4 **A** I'd love to go shopping on Saturday, but I have too much to do.
 B **a** Let me know if you change your mind. **b** I'm sorry. Unfortunately, I can't.

2 REAL-WORLD STRATEGY

SOFTENING COMMENTS

You can use *kind of* or *sort of* before adjectives to soften your comments so the other person won't feel uncomfortable.

Are you free on Saturday?

I'm sorry. Unfortunately, I'm going to be ***kind of*** *busy all weekend.*

A **Read the information in the box about softening comments. Which expression does Mari use?**

B 2.06 **Listen to a conversation between Victor and his friend Nate. What does Victor want to do? Why does Nate say "no" for Friday? Why does he say "no" for Saturday?**

C 2.06 **Listen again. What adjective does Nate use to describe heavy metal concerts? Which phrase does he use to soften his comment?**

D PAIR WORK **Practice the conversation with a partner and add phrases to soften the comments. More than one answer is possible. Change roles and practice again.**

A Do you want to see a documentary later?
B No thanks. I think documentaries are boring.
A How about a thriller?
B I'm sorry, but I'm tired.
A I understand. Let me know if you change your mind.

E PAIR WORK **Student A: Go to page 157. Student B: Go to page 158. Follow the instructions.**

3 PRONUNCIATION: Saying /m/ in *I'm*

A 2.07 **Listen. Focus on the /m/ sound in *I'm*.**

1 Sorry. I can't go. **I'm** going to a concert that night.
2 **I'm** kind of busy this week.

B 2.08 **Listen. Which speaker (A or B) says the /m/ sound? Write *A* or *B*.**

1 ___ **I'm** sorry. I can't.
2 ___ **I'm** going on a business trip that week.
3 ___ I'd love to but **I'm** kind of busy tomorrow.
4 ___ **I'm** sorry you can't go. Can we meet next week?

C **Practice the sentences in B with a partner. Does your partner say the /m/ sound in *I'm* clearly?**

4 SPEAKING

A **Think of a few events that you could invite someone to. Use an idea below or your own idea.**

a night out	a party	a sporting event
a concert	a special event	

B PAIR WORK **Invite your partner to an event. Your partner refuses your invitation. Respond to his or her refusal. Change roles and repeat.**

Do you want to go to a karaoke club tonight?

I'd love to, but I'm kind of busy.

OK. Let me know if your plans change.

7.4 NOT JUST FOR KIDS

LESSON OBJECTIVE

- write a movie review

1 READING

A **Look at the picture. What kind of movie or TV show do you think the family is watching?**

B READ FOR GIST **Read the article. What is its main argument?**

- **a** No one knows why adults like animated movies.
- **b** Adults and kids like animated movies for many reasons.
- **c** Adults don't like animated movies.

C IDENTIFY SUPPORTING DETAILS **Read the article again. What details explain why these things help adults enjoy animated movies?**

1 technology
2 real-life topics
3 humor
4 famous actors
5 endings

Animation for All Ages

Animation used to be just for kids, but today, a growing number of animated movie audiences are adults without children. What makes people of all ages enjoy animated movies these days?

Hi-tech actions Today's animated characters often look very realistic thanks to technology. The characters can walk, talk, dance, and sing almost as realistically as people can. They are also better able to show their feelings through their facial expressions, so audiences of all ages feel the characters' emotions are real and important.

Real-life situations These days, animated characters deal with real-life topics, such as moving to a new place, failure and success, friendship, growing up, and growing old. These are topics that adults can understand – even if the story is about a cat, dog, robot, or dinosaur.

Adult humor Writers include humor that both children and adults enjoy, and there are often "secret jokes" that only adults find amusing.

Well-known actors Many famous actors record the voices for animated movies nowadays. This gives star power to animated movies. Adults enjoy hearing their favorite actors bring animated characters to life.

Happy endings The biggest reason people of all ages enjoy animated movies just might be the endings. They usually end in a positive way, and everyone loves a happy ending.

We all like to laugh and have an adventure with the characters in a movie, and animated movies make that possible in a colorful and magical way.

D GROUP WORK THINK CRITICALLY **Do you think it's a good idea for writers to use adult humor in animated movies? Why or why not?**

3 WRITING

A Read Mateo's review of *Toy Story*. Is everything in the review positive? Why or why not?

MOVIE CLASSICS

Home News Reviews Sign in

Reviews & Ratings for

Toy Story

★★★★☆

One of my favorite movies ever

Author: AnimationFanMateo

[1]I didn't use to like animated movies. But after I saw *Toy Story*, I became a fan. It's one of my favorite movies ever. The story is interesting from beginning to end. [2]If you haven't seen it, it's about toys that come alive when they're alone. Six-year-old Andy's favorite toy is Woody, a cowboy. Woody is also the leader of the other toys. But then a cool, new toy arrives – a space action figure named Buzz Lightyear. He has a lot of fancy features, and Andy is fascinated. Woody hates Buzz and tries to get rid of him, but after some adventures together, the two toys become friends. [3]*Toy Story* is as dramatic as a movie with real actors, and Woody and Buzz have the same feelings as ordinary people. Their voices are perfect, especially Tom Hanks as the voice of Woody. The story has a lot of jokes for adults, so it's fun for the whole family. My only complaint is that the animation looks a little old now. Animation technology has improved a lot since 1995.

[4]But it will always be a great movie!

GLOSSARY

dramatic *(adj)* full of action and excitement

B **WRITING SKILLS** Read about organizing ideas in a movie review. Match parts 1–4 in Mateo's review with the sections below.

____ Give a brief description of the story.

____ Give a final statement with your opinion and/or a recommendation.

____ Introduce the movie and give your feeling or opinion about it.

____ Describe positive and/or negative things about the movie.

REGISTER CHECK

When we describe a movie to a friend in a text message, we usually don't worry about organization. Notice how the order of ideas in the texts is different from the order Mateo used in his more formal review.

I just saw Toy Story again.

Yeah? I've never seen it.

Really? It's famous. The main character is the voice of Tom Hanks.

Cool! Tom Hanks is always good.

Definitely! The movie's about toys that come to life. It has some good jokes.

WRITE IT

C Write a review of a movie you have seen. Organize your ideas in the same order Mateo used in his review.

D **PAIR WORK** Exchange reviews with a partner. Have you seen the movie your partner describes? Do you agree with his/her opinions? If you haven't seen it, would you like to?

7.5

TIME TO SPEAK
Changing tastes

LESSON OBJECTIVE
- talk about changing tastes

FIND IT

A **DISCUSS** With a partner, talk about some music, movies, and TV shows you used to like five years ago. Then talk about what you like today. You can go online to find out more details about entertainment five years ago.

B **DECIDE** Which profile below describes you, and which one do you think describes your partner? Compare your ideas.

Rock: Your tastes never change.

Onion: You keep all of your old tastes and also get some new ones.

Tree: You keep some of your old tastes but lose others. You also get new tastes.

Chameleon: Your tastes keep changing completely.

C **PREPARE** In your opinion, how common is each profile in your class? With your partner, make a prediction. Rank the profiles from the most common to the least common.

D **PRESENT** Tell the class about your ranking. Then everyone in the class reveals their profile. What is the most common profile in the class? The least common? Was your prediction correct?

E **AGREE** As a class, compare the opinions below with what you learned in part D. How much do you agree or disagree with them?
- We all get bored with things eventually.
- Everyone loves to discover new things.
- Our tastes depend on our age.
- Our tastes change because trends change.
- Our tastes don't change much.

To check your progress, go to page 155.

USEFUL PHRASES

DISCUSS
I used to like … , but now I don't like it so much.
I've always liked …
My favorite … is/was …

PREPARE / PRESENT
I think everyone / most people / some people …
I don't think many people / anyone …

AGREE
I think this is true.
I disagree.
I think this is partly true.
I agree that … , but I disagree that …

UNIT OBJECTIVES

- talk about what you've been doing
- talk about progress
- catch up with people's news
- write a post about managing your time
- decide on better ways to use your time

GETTING THERE

8

START SPEAKING

A **What are the people in the picture doing? Do you spend a lot of time doing this? Do you enjoy it?**

B **Talk about other things you do:**

- only because you like to.
- only because you have to.
- because you have to but also like to.

C **Imagine each day is two hours longer. With this extra time, would you do things you *want to do*, *have to do*, or both? Say what you would do. For ideas, watch Andres's video.**

What would Andres do with his extra time?

8.1 SAYING AND DOING

LESSON OBJECTIVE
- talk about what you've been doing

1 LANGUAGE IN CONTEXT

FIND IT

A GROUP WORK **Look at the sayings. What do they mean? You can go online to learn more about these sayings.**

1 Work hard, play hard.
2 No pain, no gain.
3 You only live once.
4 Variety is the spice of life.
5 Actions speak louder than words.

B 2.09 **Read and listen to three people talking about their lives. What is each person doing these days?**

C 2.09 **Read and listen again. Match a saying in exercise 1A to each person. There are two extra sayings.**

What have you been doing lately?

Vanessa

___ I have an opportunity to work in Mexico next year. I think it'll be an interesting experience, but it's going to be a challenge because I need to be able to speak the language. So, I've only been doing one thing lately – studying Spanish. It's a difficult job, so I haven't been going out at all. But that's OK. It'll be worth it.

Rodney

___ At work, I've been designing a new app. It's not easy, but I'm getting there. I think it will be a big success as well as a personal achievement for me. It's not the only thing in my life, though. I'm on a soccer team, and we're doing really well. Soccer practice is a nice change after sitting in front of a computer all day. Now I just need to make time for family and friends!

Min-hee

___ I've been doing lots of things lately! I've been painting pictures of nature – that's a fun project. I've also been learning to make sushi. It's a long process, but I'm getting better at it. And of course, I always have chores, like doing the dishes or the laundry. Yeah … it's a challenge to fit in everything I want to do. But that's what makes life interesting!

2 VOCABULARY: Describing experiences

A 2.10 **Listen and say the words. Then find and underline these nouns in the text in exercise 1C.**

achievement	challenge	change	chore	job
opportunity	process	project	success	

INSIDER ENGLISH

We use *It's worth it* and *It'll be worth it* to show that something is useful or enjoyable even though it takes a lot of effort.

B PAIR WORK **Ask and answer the questions.**

1 What is an annoying chore you have to do at home?
2 What's your biggest achievement?
3 What is one change that has happened in your life that was good?
4 Who has given you a good opportunity in the past? What was it?

C **Now go to page 148. Do the vocabulary exercises for 8.1.**

D PAIR WORK **Look at the sayings in exercise 1A. Which one do you agree with the most? Why? For ideas, watch Brenda's video.**

Which saying does Brenda talk about?

3 GRAMMAR: Present perfect continuous

A **Circle the correct answer. Use the sentences in the grammar box to help you.**

To make the present perfect continuous, use *have* + ***be*** / ***been*** + verb + *-ing*.

Present perfect continuous

What **have** you **been doing**?
I'**ve been painting** pictures of nature.
I **haven't been going out** at all.

! Use ***have, haven't, has,*** or ***hasn't*** in short answers. Do not use ***been.***
Have you been going out?
Yes, I have. / No, I haven't.

B **Complete the conversations with the correct form of the words in parentheses ( ). Then check your accuracy.**

1 **A** What ________________ lately? (you / read)
  B ________________ a lot of travel blogs. (I / read)
2 **A** ________________ recently? (you / eat out)
  B No, ________________ .
  ________________ at home. (I / cook)
3 **A** How ________________ to class these days? (you / get)
  B ________________ me to class. (my sister / drive)
4 **A** Where ________________ ? (you / study)
  B ________________ at the library lately. (I / study)

✓ ACCURACY CHECK

Remember to use the correct form of *have* with the present perfect continuous.
~~I'm having~~ been studying a lot lately. ✗
I've been studying a lot lately. ✓

C PAIR WORK **Practice the conversations from exercise 3B. Change the answers so they're true for you.**

What have you been reading lately?
I've been reading some new comic books.

D **Now go to page 136. Look at the grammar chart and do the grammar exercise for 8.1.**

4 SPEAKING

A **Think of some activities your friends or family have been doing lately. Use the topics below or your own ideas.**

child care classes hobbies housework school work

B PAIR WORK **Talk about what your friends or family have been doing recently.**

My sister has been taking karate classes.

C GROUP WORK **Work with another pair. Talk about the activities you discussed in your pairs. Whose activities are the most difficult? Whose are the most interesting?**

8.2 STARTED, BUT NOT FINISHED

LESSON OBJECTIVE
- talk about progress

1 LANGUAGE IN CONTEXT

A **Look at the picture. What is he doing? What do you do when you're out in a city?**

B **Read Monroe's social media post. What is he working on? Why is he asking his friends for advice?**

Add friends | Messages | Photos | More | Settings | Sign out

Hey friends! I've been **making good progress** on a personal project, but I need some help. Every day, I take a short video on my smartphone of something funny, strange, or beautiful in my city. I've been posting my videos on YouTube, mostly, and I've shared a few on this site, too. A lot of you have said really nice things about them – thanks! 🙂

Now, I think it's time for the next step … my own show! Really! 😉 I want to make the first episode of a show about city life. It will **concentrate on** the parts of the city most people don't see. But I haven't saved enough money to get a real video camera yet. I need people to write scripts and edit the videos, too. I've been **spending** a lot of **time** asking people for help, but no one has said "yes" yet.

Am I **wasting** my **time**, you guys? What should I do?

Like Comment Share 35 35

C **Read again. What jobs does Monroe need help with?**

2 VOCABULARY: Describing progress

FIND IT

A 2.11 PAIR WORK **Look at the pairs of sentences. Which pairs have a similar meaning? Which have an opposite or different meaning? You can use a dictionary or phone to help with words you don't know. Then listen and check.**

1 A I've been **making good progress**. B I've been **getting nowhere**.
2 A I've been **having problems with** that. B I've been **having trouble with** that.
3 A I haven't **had time** to do that. B I haven't **had a chance** to do that.
4 A I've been **doing my best**. B I've been **taking it easy**.
5 A I've been **spending** a lot of **time** doing that. B I've been **concentrating on** that.
6 A I've **wasted** a lot of **time**. B I've **saved** a lot of **time**.

B **Now go to page 148. Do the vocabulary exercises for 8.2.**

C PAIR WORK **Read the last paragraph of Monroe's post again. How does he feel right now? Talk about times when you have felt like that.**

3 GRAMMAR: Present perfect vs. present perfect continuous

A **Circle the correct answers. Use the sentences in the grammar box to help you.**

1 Use the **present perfect / present perfect continuous** to focus on the results of a finished activity.

2 Use the **present perfect / present perfect continuous** for an unfinished activity that started in the past.

Present perfect vs. present perfect continuous

Present perfect	Present perfect continuous
I'**ve shared** a few videos on this site.	I'**ve been making good progress** on a personal project.
A lot of you **have said** nice things.	I'**ve been posting** my videos.
I **haven't saved** enough money.	I'**ve been spending** a lot of **time** asking people for help.

B **Complete the paragraph with the verbs in parentheses ( ). Use the present perfect or the present perfect continuous.**

Recently, I [1] *have been trying* (try) to find a larger apartment. It's not easy. I [2] ________ (look) at ads for a few weeks, and I [3] ________ (visit) two places so far. I [4] ________ (think) about which one to rent, but I [5] ________ (not decide) yet. Actually, I'm not really sure I want to move. I [6] ________ (live) in my present apartment for just eight months, so maybe I should stay here a little longer.

C PAIR WORK **Talk about something you've been thinking about spending money on. Say what you've looked at so far and what you've found out.**

D **Now go to page 136. Look at the grammar chart and do the grammar exercise for 8.2.**

4 SPEAKING

A **Think about something you've been working on lately, but haven't finished. Use one of the topics below or your own ideas.**

art	clubs	family	hobbies
school	volunteering	work	

B PAIR WORK **Talk about the things you've been working on. What have you been doing? What have you done so far? What haven't you done yet?**

I've been spending a lot of time on work for college. I've been concentrating on a project for my psychology class. So far, I've only written about two pages. I've been having trouble finding the information I need.

8.3 HOW HAVE YOU BEEN?

LESSON OBJECTIVE
- catch up with people's news

1 FUNCTIONAL LANGUAGE

A 2.12 **Look at the picture. The women haven't seen each other for a long time. What do you think they're talking about? Then read and listen to their conversation. What topics do they mention?**

2.12 Audio script

A It's great to see you again, Juliet. **It's been a long time.**

B I know. **I haven't seen you since** last spring. That was the last time I was here in Mexicali for work.

A I'm so happy you could meet me today. So, **what have you been up to**?

B Oh, **the same as usual**. Working, going to the gym, seeing friends. **What have you been doing**?

A **I've been really busy.** I got a new job in January, so …

B Hey, congratulations!

A Thanks. It's great, but there's one problem. We start work at 8:00, so I've been getting up at 6:00 every morning. Can you believe it?

B No! I remember you hated getting up early in college. By the way, how's your brother, Antonio? **What's going on with him**?

A **Not much**. He's on vacation right now. But listen. Why don't we go and have lunch together, and you can tell me all your news? I know a great Chinese restaurant.

B Really? I love Chinese food, but … we're in Mexico!

A Didn't you know that Mexicali is famous for its Chinese restaurants?

B **Complete the chart with expressions in bold from the conversation above.**

Saying how long it's been	Asking about someone's news	Answering
[1] ______ a long time. I [2] ______ last spring. / for a long time.	What [3] ______ up to? What have you [4] ______? [5] ______ him? How have you been?	The same [6] ______. [7] ______ (really) busy. Not [8] ______.

C 2.13 **Choose the correct responses. Then listen and check.**

1	Wow! It's been a long time.	**a** Yeah. What have you been doing?	**b** The same as usual.
2	What have you been up to?	**a** What have you been doing?	**b** Not much.
3	What's going on with Peter?	**a** He's really busy.	**b** It's been a long time.
4	I haven't seen you for a long time.	**a** I know. How have you been?	**b** The same as usual.

2 REAL-WORLD STRATEGY

A 2.14 **Listen to more of Rosa and Juliet's conversation. What does Rosa suggest? What does Juliet ask?**

B 2.14 **Read the information in the box about using *That would be* to comment on something. Then listen again. What comment does Juliet make?**

USING *THAT WOULD BE* TO COMMENT ON SOMETHING

You can use *That would be* (or *That'd be*) and an adjective to comment on a suggestion or possibility.

Why don't we go and have lunch together? I know a great Chinese restaurant.

*Really? **That would be great!** I love Chinese food.*

C 2.15 **Listen and complete the conversation with an adjective. Then practice with a partner.**

A Lenny got another speeding ticket. His parents are thinking about taking away his car.

B That would be ________________ ! He loves his car.

D PAIR WORK **Student A: Go to page 157. Student B: Go to page 158. Follow the instructions.**

3 PRONUNCIATION: Saying /ɑ/ and /æ/ vowel sounds

A 2.16 **Listen and repeat the two different vowel sounds.**

/ɑ/ got Lenny got another speeding ticket.
/æ/ haven't I haven't seen you since last spring.

B 2.17 **Listen. Write A for words with /ɑ/. Write B for words with /æ/.**

1 ___ can
2 ___ haven't
3 ___ concentrate
4 ___ problem
5 ___ job
6 ___ chance

C PAIR WORK **Practice the words from exercise 3B with a partner. Does your partner say the /ɑ/ and /æ/ sounds?**

4 SPEAKING

A PAIR WORK **Imagine you are friends who haven't seen each other in a long time. Ask and answer the questions below. You can answer with your own information or make something up.**

- How've you been?
- What have you been up to?
- What's going on with … ?

B PAIR WORK **Continue the conversation. Suggest something you can do together, and agree on one of the ideas.**

Why don't we go get coffee? I would love to catch up. There's a nice espresso place on the corner.

Really? That would be great! I could use a coffee.

8.4 A TIME-SAVING TIP

LESSON OBJECTIVE
- write a post about managing your time

1 LISTENING

A **Look at the pictures. Which activity takes the most time? Which one takes the least amount of time?**

B 2.18 LISTEN FOR EXAMPLES **Listen to the podcast. What two small activities does Naomi talk about?**

C 2.18 GUESS MEANING FROM CONTEXT **Listen again. What do these words mean?**

1 **wisely**	a in a boring way	b in a smart way	c in an exciting way
2 **technique**	a a place to go	b a difficult process	c a way of doing something
3 **responded**	a answered someone	b asked something	c didn't understand someone
4 **tasks**	a times you have to be somewhere	b things you have to do	c places you go to work
5 **as well as**	a and	b but	c so

2 PRONUNCIATION: Listening for weak forms of *didn't*

A 2.19 **Listen to the extracts from the podcast. Focus on how the speaker says the words in bold.**

1 It **didn't** take very long.
2 Then I **didn't** need to put those tasks on my to-do list.

B 2.20 **Listen. Which speaker (A or B) says *didn't* like the speakers in A? Write *A* or *B*.**

1 ___ I didn't know how much time I was wasting.
2 ___ I could have answered the emails right away, but I didn't.
3 ___ I didn't realize paying my bills online was so easy.
4 ___ It didn't take as much time as I thought.

C **Check (✓) the statement that is true.**

☐ In fast speech, English speakers often drop the /d/ sound at the beginning of *didn't*.
☐ In fast speech, English speakers often drop the /t/ sound at the end of *didn't*.

3 WRITING

A Read the post Matthew wrote on the Tools for Life podcast website. What has he achieved since the podcast? Why didn't he do these things in the past?

Home News Radio Podcasts Community Sign in

Tools *for* Life

Episode 201: Interview with Naomi Moore

Subscribe Listen

Comments

Matthew, Chicago
6 hours ago

After I heard this podcast, I knew I had to try Naomi's technique. I don't have many problems with emails, but I do have a lot of homework! Up to now I've had a lot of trouble managing all the work for my different classes. To be honest, sometimes I don't prepare for class as much as I should because I'm tired or busy, or have something better to do. But I always felt worried and stressed about it.

So I sat down and made a to-do list. Even that was a little frightening! I put all the jobs into two groups: short jobs (that I could do in less than five minutes) and long jobs. I immediately started with a few short jobs – I put away my papers, cleaned my desk, and things like that. I felt much happier right away. I had so much energy, I worked on one of my "long jobs" afterward – I wrote an outline for a research paper that's due next week.

So far, this has been working well! I feel more positive about what's on my to-do list. From now on, I'm going to try to study a little every day, and I'll probably finish my research paper early next week. If you're stressed about organization, definitely try Naomi's plan!!

Like 7 Reply Share Report

B PAIR WORK THINK CRITICALLY How has this technique changed Matthew's life? Do you think he'll continue to make improvements? Why or why not?

C WRITING SKILLS Read the information about time expressions and match the time expressions (1–4) with ones of the same meaning (a–d). Then find and underline some of the time expressions in Matthew's post.

Use time expressions to talk about actions and experiences in the present, past, and future.

1	immediately ___	a	up to now
2	so far ___	b	from now on
3	before ___	c	right away
4	in the future ___	d	in the past

REGISTER CHECK

We often put time phrases at the beginning of sentences in more formal writing. In informal writing, we often put them at the end.

Formal: *From now on, I'm going to try to study a little every day.*

Informal: *I'm going to try to study a little every day from now on.*

WRITE IT

D Write a post about how you manage your time and the things you have to do. If you already use Naomi's technique (or a similar one), describe your experiences. If you don't use a time-management technique, describe how you've been managing up to now and say what you might do in the future to manage your time better.

E PAIR WORK Exchange posts with a partner. Would you like to use any of your partner's time-management ideas?

8.5 TIME TO SPEAK
Building a better life

LESSON OBJECTIVE
- decide on better ways to use your time

A **PREPARE** Look at the words below. Which things make you happy, and which ones don't? Write them in the pyramid above, with the things you like best at the top and things you like least at the bottom.

chores	commuting	exercise	family	free-time activities
friends	learning	rest	travel	work

B **DECIDE** Share your pyramid with your partner. Discuss how you've been spending your time lately and compare it with the information in your pyramid. Then each decide on two things you'd like to spend more time on and two things you'd like to spend less time on.

C **DISCUSS** In groups, share the things you want to spend more time on and less time on. Give each other advice on how to make these changes in your lives. Your ideas can be big, small, serious, or funny. Be creative!

D **PRESENT** Tell the class about the best advice you got from your group in part C.

E **AGREE** As a class, choose the three most creative ideas you heard in part D.

To check your progress, go to page 155.

USEFUL PHRASES

PREPARE
... makes me happy.
I enjoy ...
I don't really like ...
I'm not interested in ...

DECIDE
I've been spending a lot of time ...
I haven't had (much) time to ...

DISCUSS
I want to spend more/less time ...
You could ... Or you could ...
What about ... ing ... ?

UNIT OBJECTIVES

- talk about college subjects
- discuss rules for working and studying at home
- express confidence and lack of confidence
- write the main part of a résumé
- decide how to use your skills

MAKE IT WORK

9

START SPEAKING

A Where do you think this man is working? Do you know anyone that works from an unusual place? Why?

B What kind of job do you think this man does? What other jobs allow people to telecommute?

C Discuss the pros and cons of working like this. Would you like it? Why or why not?

D Do you think the man is telecommuting because he *chooses to* or because he *has to*? How much choice do most people have about where or how they work or study? For ideas, watch Angie's video.

REAL STUDENT

Does Angie have the same ideas you do?

9.1 BUILDING A FUTURE

LESSON OBJECTIVE
- talk about college subjects

1 VOCABULARY: College subjects

A 2.21 PAIR WORK **Listen and say the words. Give an example of something students learn about in each college subject.**

architecture, biology, business
chemistry, computer science, economics
education, engineering, law
medicine, physics, political science

B PAIR WORK **Which are your favorite subjects? Which are you not interested in? Why?**

C **Now go to page 149. Do the vocabulary exercises for 9.1.**

2 LANGUAGE IN CONTEXT

A PAIR WORK **What jobs do you think the subjects in exercise 1A are useful for? Why?**

B 2.22 **Read and listen to the conversation between two cousins. Have they thought about their future jobs? What are they going to do?**

2.22 Audio script

Ian So, when will you start training as a mechanic?

Luca Well, actually, I'm going to get a degree in automotive **engineering** instead.

Ian Why do you need to get a degree? I thought you were going to work in your dad's garage.

Luca I am. But Dad says I have to get a degree first. Anyway, what about you?

Ian I'm going to create my own program of study. I want to take courses in **business**, **education**, and maybe **biology**.

Luca Wow, that's an interesting mix! But don't you have to choose a major?

Ian No. It's like I'm creating my own major. Here, this is from the college website: "Applicants must take 120 credits of any subject to get a degree."

Luca Interesting. So, what kind of job do you want to get after that?

Ian For now, I'm going to take classes I like and see how it goes. I don't have to choose a job yet.

Luca True. Well, with a degree like that, I guess you'll be ready for anything!

GLOSSARY
degree *(n)* a qualification you get for finishing college
major *(n)* the most important part of your study in college

C 2.22 **Read and listen again. How is Ian's program different from Luca's?**

D PAIR WORK **Would you like to create your own major? Why or why not? For ideas, watch Andrea's video.**

INSIDER ENGLISH

We use *see how it goes* to say we will allow a situation to develop for some time before we make a decision.

REAL STUDENT

What kind of program of study does Andrea want?

3 GRAMMAR: Modals of necessity: *have to, need to, must*

A **Circle the correct answers. Use the sentences in the grammar box to help you.**

1 Use *have to, need to*, or *must* to say something is **necessary** / **not necessary**.

2 Use *don't have to* or *don't need to* to say something is **necessary** / **not necessary**.

3 After *have to, need to*, or *must*, use the **base form** / **-*ing* form** of the verb.

Modals of necessity: *have to, need to, must*

I **have to get** a degree first.
I **don't have to choose** a job yet.
Applicants **must take** 120 credits of any subject to get a degree.
Why do you **need to get** a degree?
Don't you **have to choose** a major?

B **Complete the sentences with the correct forms of the words in parentheses ( ). Use the simple present. Then tell a partner if you agree with the sentences.**

1 You ______________ (not have to / work) hard to be successful.

2 When you ______________ (need to / shop) for clothes, it's best to order them online.

3 You ______________ (need to / think) about what job you want in the future and then choose what to study.

4 I ______________ (have to / do) a lot of chores, but most of them are a waste of time.

C Now go to page 137. Look at the grammar chart and do the grammar exercise for 9.1.

D **Complete the sentences with your own ideas. Then share with a partner.**

1 When I was in school, I had to ______________ .

2 Now, I don't need to ______________ .

3 To be successful, college students need to ______________ .

4 In my country, students don't have to ______________ .

4 SPEAKING

A **Think of a job you want to have. What do you need to learn to get this job? Make a list of three subjects. Think about how you could learn these subjects.**

B PAIR WORK **Compare your lists and talk about how you will learn these subjects. What do you think will happen when you learn them?**

I want to be an architect. I'm really interested in cool buildings.

You probably need to take art classes.

C GROUP WORK **Join another pair. Make a plan for your group to learn your new subjects. Whose subjects are more interesting? Whose subjects seem harder? Can you think of creative ways to use your new knowledge?**

9.2 HOUSE RULES

LESSON OBJECTIVE
- discuss rules for working and studying at home

1 LANGUAGE IN CONTEXT

A **Look at the picture of a self-employed woman. What do you think is good about working from home? What's difficult?**

B **Read the posts on an internet forum. What two things does Rina want help with?**

C **Read again. Summarize what Theo, Lynn, and Kosuke suggest.**

Posted at 10:02 a.m.

Rina I just started my own small business and am working from home. I need to make some rules for myself. Any suggestions?

Theo You have to imagine you're going to an office. Get up, get dressed, and have the same working hours every day. You can take short breaks, of course, but you can't waste time. For example, you shouldn't do chores during working hours because you'll never get your work done. And you must not miss your deadlines!

Lynn Make time for yourself. You can't spend all of your time on work. Sometimes, it's hard to stop working when your office is in your home.

Rina Thanks! I see it's going to be important to manage my time. Now, any tips on how to manage my files? I work for a lot of different employers, and my wages are different for each contract.

Kosuke There are a lot of great computer programs to help you with that kind of thing.

Rina Thanks, Kosuke. May I email you? I'd love to chat more about those programs.

Kosuke Of course! My #1 rule for working at home: Get help when you can!

GLOSSARY
deadline *(n)* a time or day by which something must be done

2 VOCABULARY: Employment

FIND IT

A 2.23 **Find and underline six of these words in the posts in exercise 1C. Then write all of the words in the correct places in the chart and discuss what they mean. You can use a dictionary or your phone to look up words you don't know. Then listen and check.**

apply career contract employer fire hire
manage profession retirement salary wage working hours

Nouns		Verbs	

B **Now go to page 149. Do the vocabulary exercises for 9.2.**

C GROUP WORK **Which problem do you think is worse for people who work at home – not working enough or working too much? Why?**

3 GRAMMAR: Modals of prohibition and permission

A **Circle the correct answers. Use the sentences in the grammar box to help you.**

1 Use *can't* or *must not* to say you **are** / **aren't** allowed to do something.

2 Use *can*, *may*, or *could* to say you **are** / **aren't** allowed to do something.

Modals of prohibition and permission

Prohibition: *can't*, *must not*	Permission: *can*, *may*, *could*
You **can't waste** time.	You **can take** short breaks.
You **must not miss** your deadlines.	**May** I **email** you?

! ***Must not*** **does not have the same meaning as** ***don't have to***. ***Must not*** **means you can't do something.** ***Don't have to*** **means you can do something, but it's not necessary.**

B **Circle the correct answers. Check your accuracy. Then practice the conversation with a partner. Do you agree with Mario or Sarah about working from home on Fridays?**

Mario I heard that we can work from home on Fridays now. [1]*Can* / *Must* we work any hours we want?

Sarah No, we [2]*may* / *can't*. We have to work from 9:00 a.m. to 5:00 p.m.

Mario I guess we [3]*can* / *must not* take breaks, though.

Sarah Yeah, but you have to log in and [4]*can* / *can't* stop working for more than 15 minutes at a time – except at lunchtime. And the boss's email also says, "You [5]*could* / *must not* use your computer for personal use." Our computers know everything.

Mario And they tell the boss! But it's still great that we [6]*can* / *could* work from home.

Sarah I don't know. I think we're going to have to work harder than in the office.

✓ ACCURACY CHECK

You can use ***could*** **to ask for permission, but not to give someone permission.**

Could I email you? ✓

~~Yes, you could email me.~~ ✗

D **Now go to page 137. Look at the grammar chart and do the grammar exercise for 9.2.**

E **Complete the sentences with your own ideas.**

1 When you study at the library, you must not ________________ .

2 If you study with me at my house, you can't ________________ , but you can ________________ .

3 Can I ________________ after class?

4 SPEAKING

A **Make a list of rules for working or studying at home. Think of as many ideas as you can. Be creative!**

B PAIR WORK **Compare your lists. Then choose your three best ideas.**

You can't have a lot of snacks in the house when you work from home. You'll eat all day and not get anything done!

True. But you can take breaks for meals. And you need to eat away from your desk.

C GROUP WORK **Present your three ideas to another pair. Which ideas are the most helpful?**

9.3 A NEW CHALLENGE

LESSON OBJECTIVE
- express confidence and lack of confidence

1 FUNCTIONAL LANGUAGE

A 2.24 PAIR WORK **Look at the picture of a jujitsu class. Say why someone might be worried about starting jujitsu. Then read and listen to two coworkers talking about the class. What is the woman worried about? How does the man respond?**

2.24 Audio script

A I heard you're giving jujitsu lessons to some of our coworkers.
B I am. We're starting next week. Why don't you join us?
A Me, doing jujitsu? **I'm not sure I can handle** that!
B Why not?
A **I don't think I'm** strong **enough**.
B It's not about being strong, it's about technique. And if you're worried about falling …
A Well, yeah. **That concerns me** a little!
B Honestly, **that won't be a problem**. You'll learn to fall safely. And it's a beginners' group.
A OK. And who's in the group?
B Well, if you join us, you'll have to fight with your boss!
A Well, **that doesn't bother me. I think I can handle** that!

B **Complete the chart with expressions in bold from the conversation.**

Expressing confidence	Expressing lack of confidence
That won't [1] ______________ .	I'm not sure [4] ______________ that.
That doesn't [2] ______________ .	I don't think I'm strong [5] ______________ .
I think [3] ______________ that.	That [6] ______________ a little.

C PAIR WORK **For each sentence, choose a response from the chart in exercise 1B to say how you feel. Then practice the conversations with a partner.**

1 The pilot is sick. You need to fly the plane and land it!
2 We're inviting 15 people to the barbecue. Can you make all the food?
3 For your English test, you'll need to write five sentences in the simple past.
4 On the team-building course, you'll have to hike 25 miles (40 km) in the mountains.

2 REAL-WORLD STRATEGY

A 2.25 **Listen to the conversation. What does Robin invite Tim to do? Does he accept?**

B 2.25 **Read the information in the box about focusing on reasons. Then listen again. What's the reason why Tim doesn't like mountain biking?**

FOCUSING ON REASONS

You can use *The thing is* to focus on the reason why you don't want to or can't do something.

Me, doing jujitsu? I'm not sure I can handle that! ***The thing is,*** *I'm not very strong.*

C **Complete the conversation with a reason why you can't go swimming. Then practice the conversation with a partner. Who gave the best reason?**

A Would you like to go swimming with me on Sunday morning?

B Thanks for the offer, but I can't. ______________________

D PAIR WORK **Student A: Go to page 157. Student B: Go to page 158. Follow the instructions.**

3 PRONUNCIATION: Grouping words

A 2.26 **Listen and repeat. Focus on how words are grouped.**

A I don't think / I'm strong / enough.

B It's not about / being strong, / it's about / technique.

B 2.27 **Group the words in the conversation. Mark the groups with a /. Then listen and check.**

A Would you like to go swimming with me on Sunday morning?

B Thanks for the offer, but I can't. I'm taking my sister to breakfast for her birthday.

A OK. Well, I go every Sunday morning. What about the next Sunday?

C PAIR WORK **Work with a partner. Practice the conversation in B with a partner. Does your partner say the word groups correctly?**

4 SPEAKING

A **Think of some challenging sports or outdoor activities that people can do in or near your city. Make notes.**

B PAIR WORK **Use your ideas to plan a weekend challenge for a group of people. Choose one activity for Saturday morning and one for Saturday afternoon.**

C GROUP WORK **Tell other pairs about your plan. They say whether or not they can handle the activities and say if they'd like to join your group.**

So, in the morning we're going to go skateboarding at the skate park.

That won't be a problem. I used to skateboard when I was a kid.

I'm not sure I can handle that. The thing is, my legs aren't very strong.

9.4 A JOB SEARCH

LESSON OBJECTIVE
- write the main part of a résumé

1 READING

FIND IT

A **RECOGNIZE TEXT TYPES** **Look at the two texts. What is each one from? Choose from the words in the box. You can use a dictionary or your phone to help with words you don't know.**

a cover letter	a guidebook	a job ad
a job application	a passport application	a résumé

CareerQuest.com

Local Jobs | Search Jobs | Events | Résumé Help | Join | Log In

Description:
We're looking for someone reliable and intelligent to join our growing team. The perfect applicant is ready for a new challenge. This is an excellent opportunity if you're interested in a "people profession." Salary is based on experience.

Responsibilities:
You will help us design our programs and increase our business. You must be able to deal with difficult customers calmly. Working hours are usually from 9:00 a.m. to 5:00 p.m., but you also have to work two evenings a week.

Qualifications:
You need to have a two-year or four-year degree in education, business, or similar. You should have at least two years of work experience. You need strong communication skills and basic computer skills, and you must write well. You need to work well in a group and by yourself.

APPLY NOW

GLOSSARY
applicant *(n)* a person who applies for a job
qualifications *(n)* skills or experiences that prepare you to do a job or activity

Jacob Bradley

298 Willow Street, Denver, Colorado 80123
303-555-2910
jbradley23@metmail.com

PROFESSIONAL PROFILE

I have a degree in education with one year of experience as a teacher's assistant at a high school. I'm bilingual (English and Spanish). My biggest accomplishment so far is starting an after-school technology program for teens. I'm also a soccer coach, and I play on a basketball team. I learn new things quickly and get along well with people of all ages.

EXPERIENCE

B **READ FOR DETAILS** **Read both texts. Answer the questions.**

1 What kind of person does the employer want to hire?
2 If the person is hired, when will he or she have to work?
3 Compare Jacob's profile with the qualifications needed. Do you think he should apply for the job?

C **PAIR WORK** **THINK CRITICALLY** **Look at the first text again. What do you think the job is? You can think of several possibilities.**

2 WRITING

A Read the rest of Jacob Bradley's résumé. What are the four main sections? What jobs has he had? Which one does he still have?

EXPERIENCE

Teacher's Assistant, Fairmount High School, Denver, CO
- Help plan and teach business and English classes to students in grades 10–12
- Organize classroom projects and day trips for the students

Barista, Carlo's Coffee, Denver, CO
- Prepared hot and cold drinks for customers
- Cleaned machines, work areas, and customer seating areas

EDUCATION
- Bachelor of Arts in Education, University of Colorado Boulder

SKILLS
- Fluent in English and Spanish; beginner-level Japanese
- Experienced in MS Office, Adobe Photoshop, web design
- Excellent time-management and communication skills

ACTIVITIES
- Coach, Soccer for Kids (neighborhood program)
- Member, Hoops Community Basketball

B WRITING SKILLS **Read about how to write a résumé. Then look at Jacob's résumé in exercise 2A and check (✓) the things he has done. What has he not done?**

- [ ] Use present verbs to describe a current job and past verbs to describe past jobs.
- [ ] Include dates for your past jobs, and put the most recent one first.
- [ ] Use bullet points and incomplete sentences (with no subject).
- [ ] List your degrees or certificates. Include dates, and put the most recent ones first.
- [ ] List skills that are useful for jobs. They can be skills you learned or personal skills.
- [ ] List activities and interests that show you are active, creative, or good with people.

REGISTER CHECK

In résumé writing, people often use parallel structures in bulleted lists.

Simple present verbs	Simple past verbs	Nouns to describe positions/people
– *Help plan and teach …*	– *Prepared hot and cold drinks …*	– *Coach, Soccer for Kids …*
– *Organize classroom projects …*	– *Cleaned machines …*	– *Member, Hoops Community …*

WRITE IT

C **Write the main part of a résumé. Begin with EXPERIENCE and end with ACTIVITIES. You can include real information or make it up. Follow the rules in exercise 2B and use parallel structures under each heading.**

D PAIR WORK **Exchange résumés with a partner. Ask your partner about one item from each of their resume sections: Experience, Education, Skills, and Activities. Do you have anything surprising in common?**

9.5

TIME TO SPEAK
Design your perfect job

LESSON OBJECTIVE
- decide how to use your skills

A **DISCUSS** With a partner, talk about the skills and interests you need for your job – or a job you'd like to do. Compare them with your partner's job.

In engineering, you have to be good at math and physics. And you need to be interested in technology and computers.

In accounting, you have to be good at math, but you don't need to know about physics. You also …

FIND IT

B **RESEARCH** Now tell your partner about skills and interests you have, which you don't need for the job you chose in part A. Together, think of other jobs you could do in order to use these skills. You can go online to find the names of jobs you don't know in English.

I'm good at cooking. And I really like writing.

OK. So, you could be a journalist who writes about food and restaurants.

C **PREPARE** With your partner, design a real or imaginary job for each of you that uses as many of your skills and interests as possible. Invent a title for your job.

D **PRESENT** Tell the class about your partner's job and why it would be perfect for him/her.

E **AGREE** The class chooses: (a) the most useful job, (b) the most amusing job, and (c) the coolest job.

To check your progress, go to page 155.

USEFUL PHRASES

DISCUSS
You have to be good at …
You need to know a lot about …
You have to be interested in …

RESEARCH / PREPARE
You could make/help/sell/design …
You could be a / work in a …

PRESENT
My partner's job is …
It would be perfect for him/her because …

REVIEW 3 (UNITS 7–9)

1 VOCABULARY

A **Complete the chart with the words and phrases below. Then write a category name for each group.**

career	challenge	drama	EDM	education
hip-hop	jazz	opportunity	physics	political science
reality show	retirement	soap opera	success	wage

classical	game show	achievement	chemistry	profession

B **Add at least two more words or phrases to each group.**

2 GRAMMAR

A **Circle the correct words to complete the conversation.**

A 1 *Can / Must* I change the channel? I really don't like scary movies.

B Me either. I 2 *usually liked / used to like* horror movies a lot when I was a teenager, but not anymore. New horror movies are not 3 *as good as / as better as* old ones.

A I agree. By the way, have you 4 *seen / been seeing* any good movies recently?

B Well, I 5 *don't go / haven't been* to the movies in such a long time. 6 *I work / I've been working* so hard lately. 7 *I visited / I've been visiting* clients almost every day. I think 8 *I've visited / I've been visiting* about 20 clients this month.

A You 9 *need to / must* have some fun. Your social life is 10 *as important as / more important as* your job. Anyway, you 12 *didn't use / didn't used* to be so serious about work in the past.

B I know, but in the past, I wasn't a father, so I 13 *didn't have to / hadn't to* worry about the future … And hey, I do have a social life – watching TV with you!

B PAIR WORK **Has your taste in movies changed since you were younger? What kinds of movies did you use to watch? What do you watch today?**

3 SPEAKING

PAIR WORK **Talk to your partner about one of these topics. Answer your partner's questions and give as many details as possible.**

- Choose a real or invented thing you have been doing a lot lately that makes you happy. Talk to your partner about it. Give and get details.
- Choose a real or invented thing you have been doing that you're not happy about. Why have you been doing it?

> I've been learning to surf. I've been taking lessons since the beginning of summer. I've already made some progress, but I have to practice a lot more …

4 FUNCTIONAL LANGUAGE

A **Complete the conversation with the phrases below.**

a long time	be a problem	been up to	have you been	I'd love to
if you change	I haven't seen you	I'm not sure	I understand	I've been
kind of	not much	thanks for asking	the thing is	too bad

A Dmitri? Wow. Is that you?

B Raheem! [1] ______________ since we graduated.

A Yeah. It's been [2] ______________ .

B What have you [3] ______________ ?

A [4] ______________ . Working, playing tennis … What about you? What [5] ______________ doing?

B [6] ______________ really busy. I went back to school, so I've been working and studying.

A Nice! Hey, do you still play tennis? I'm on my way to the gym now. Come with me, and we can play together.

B [7] ______________ I can handle that. I haven't played for about three years.

A That won't [8] ______________ . We can take it easy.

B [9] ______________ , I broke my arm three years ago, and I stopped playing. But [10] ______________ .

A [11] ______________ . Look, some friends are coming over for dinner on Saturday. Would you like to join us?

B [12] ______________ , but I can't. Actually, I'm going to be [13] ______________ busy this weekend. I have to study for my exams.

A That's [14] ______________ . Let me know [15] ______________ your mind.

5 SPEAKING

A PAIR WORK **Choose one of the situations below. Act it out in pairs.**

- You have a job interview tomorrow, but you don't feel very confident about it. Talk to your partner and describe how you feel. Go to page 90 for useful language.

I don't think I'm prepared for my job interview tomorrow.

Why not? You have so much experience.

That won't be a problem. The thing is, I don't know much about the company …

- You and your partner were classmates a year ago. You haven't seen each other since that time. Talk about what the two of you have been doing. Go to page 80 for useful language.

It's been a long time. What have you been doing?

The same as usual. I've been …

- You're painting your apartment this weekend. Invite your partner to have lunch and then help you with the job. Go to page 70 for useful language.

I'm painting my apartment this weekend. Would you like to come for lunch and help me?

I'm sorry. Unfortunately, …

B **Change roles and repeat the role play.**

UNIT OBJECTIVES

- say what things are made of
- talk about where things come from
- question or approve of someone's choices
- write feedback about company products
- design a commercial

WHY WE BUY

10

START SPEAKING

FIND IT

A Imagine you're in this store. Would you buy any candy? What kinds? You can go online to learn the words for different kinds of candy in English.

B How did you decide which candy to buy, and how much? Do you think the child is choosing his candy for the same reasons? Do you think adults and children make decisions about what to buy for the same reasons? Why or why not?

C Think of something you bought recently. Explain why you decided to buy it. For ideas, watch Andrea's video.

REAL STUDENT

What did Andrea buy? Were any of her reasons similar to yours?

10.1 GREEN CLOTHES

LESSON OBJECTIVE
- say what things are made of

1 VOCABULARY: Describing materials

A 2.28 PAIR WORK **Listen and say the words for materials. Then look at the picture. Which of these materials do you see? What other things do we wear that use these materials?**

cotton	glass	leather	metal	plastic
polyester	stone	wood	wool	

B 2.29 **Listen and say the adjectives. Which are opposites? Which describe something the man is wearing?**

artificial	fragile	hard	heavy	light
natural	soft	strong	warm	waterproof

C **Now go to page 150. Do the vocabulary exercises for 10.1.**

INSIDER ENGLISH

We use *-friendly* with a noun to say that something is not harmful or that it's appropriate for a specific group of people. Common expressions with *-friendly* are eco-friendly, budget-friendly, family-friendly, customer-friendly, and earth-friendly.

2 LANGUAGE IN CONTEXT

A **Read the text from a clothing company's website. What questions does it ask? Which ones can you answer?**

B **Read again. Which material is more environmentally friendly: cotton or polyester? Why?**

Eco Stitch

Women | Men | Kids | Sale | About us

Shopping cart

Search

Are your clothes "green"?

For many of the things we buy, like paper products and cars, we know what's green and what's not. That knowledge helps us make eco-friendly choices. Our goal at Eco Stitch is to help you do the same with your clothing.

Unless you're wearing that **wool** sweater your grandmother knitted, you might not know what your clothes are made of. The names of the materials are written on the labels, but have you ever looked at them? Most people are interested in how fashionable the clothes are, not whether they're **cotton** or **polyester**.

Even if you know what materials you're wearing, do you know how eco-friendly they are? Cotton is taken from plants, and because it's **natural**, many people think it is more environmentally friendly than polyester, which is **artificial**. However, a lot of chemicals are used by most cotton farmers, and large amounts of water are needed, too. Meanwhile, polyester is often made from recycled **plastic** bottles. It's also **warmer** and **lighter** than cotton, so less material is needed!

We're here to help you make the best choices for you. LEARN MORE.

GLOSSARY

green *(adj)* environmentally-friendly

eco-friendly *(n)* good for the environment

C PAIR WORK **Do you know what materials your clothes are made of? Is it important to you? For ideas, watch Angie's video.**

REAL STUDENT

Do you and Angie wear similar things?

3 GRAMMAR: Simple present passive

A **Circle the correct answers. Use the sentences in the grammar box to help you.**

1 In the passive, we **always** / **sometimes** say who or what does the action.

2 For the simple present form of the passive, use *is* or *are* + **a simple present verb** / **a past participle**.

Simple present passive

Cotton **is taken** from plants.

Large amounts of water **are needed**.

! **We can use *by* to show who does the action.**

A lot of chemicals ***are used*** ***by*** *cotton farmers.*

B **Now go to page 138. Look at the grammar chart and do the grammar exercise for 10.1.**

C PAIR WORK **Complete the sentences with the simple present passive of the verbs in parentheses ( ). Then discuss whether each sentence is true for your country.**

1 Warm clothes ______ for more than half of the year. (need)

2 A lot of clothes ______ in supermarkets. (sell)

3 Jeans ______ more often than other kinds of pants. (buy)

4 Hats ______ by a lot people. (wear)

5 Most coats ______ of waterproof material. (make)

6 Most of the labels on clothes ______ in English. (write)

4 SPEAKING

FIND IT

A PAIR WORK **Think of ways the materials below are used. Make notes. You can go online to learn more.**

cotton glass plastic wood

B PAIR WORK **Are the materials in exercise 4A good or bad for the environment? To explain why, say how each material is used.**

Plastic is really bad. So many things are made of plastic – like bottles. And they're just thrown away.

That's true, but some bottles are recycled. And plastic bottles are lighter than glass bottles, so it takes less energy to transport them on trucks.

C CLASS ACTIVITY **Compare your ideas with others in the class. What did you learn about the materials?**

10.2 GLOBAL OR LOCAL?

LESSON OBJECTIVE
- talk about where things come from

1 LANGUAGE IN CONTEXT

A PAIR WORK **Look at the picture. What products and food items do you see? Guess where they came from.**

B 2.30 **Read and listen. Lucy, an economics student, is interviewing Monty. Where does Monty think his laptop, coffee, and sandwich come from? Are his ideas the same as yours?**

2.30 Audio script

Lucy Thanks for helping me with my project, Monty. So, my first question is, do you know where your laptop comes from?

Monty Well, it's an American brand, but it probably wasn't made in the US. I guess it was designed there and then manufactured in China. But I didn't think about that when I bought it. I just wanted a good laptop for a good price.

Lucy I understand. And how about your coffee?

Monty I guess the coffee beans were imported. They weren't grown here in Canada, that's for sure! They were probably shipped from Brazil. I think that's where some of the best coffee comes from, and this is really good.

Lucy Yeah. And how about your sandwich?

Monty Well, I know it's fresh because it was made right in front of me. I'm not sure about the things in it, though. The tuna was probably caught and frozen weeks ago, but maybe the tomatoes were grown here. I hope so. It's good when fruit and vegetables are produced locally.

Lucy OK, thanks very much. I think I'll get one of those sandwiches now. Talking about food always makes me hungry!

C 2.30 **Read and listen again. Why did Monty buy his laptop? What does he know for sure about his sandwich?**

GLOSSARY
brand *(n)* a product that is made by a particular company

2 VOCABULARY: Production and distribution

A 2.31 **Listen and repeat the verbs. Find and underline eight of these verbs in the interview in exercise 1B. Then answer the questions.**

catch	deliver	design	export	freeze	grow	import
manufacture	pick	produce	ship	store	transport	

Which words are about:

1 moving products from one place to another?
2 creating and making things?
3 getting fish? getting fruit?
4 keeping things for a long time?

B Now go to page 150. Do the vocabulary exercises for 10.2.

C PAIR WORK **Talk about …**

1 three kinds of food people grow or pick in your country.
2 three things that companies in your country design or manufacture.
3 three things your country exports and three things it imports.

3 GRAMMAR: Simple past passive

A **Circle the correct answers. Use the sentences in the grammar box to help you.**

1 For the simple past form of the passive, use *was* or *were* + **a past participle / a simple past verb**.

2 In questions and negative sentences, **use / do not use** *did* or *didn't*.

Simple past passive

The tuna **was caught** weeks ago.	My laptop **wasn't made** in the US.
The coffee beans **were imported**.	The beans **weren't grown** in Canada.

B **Complete the paragraphs with the simple past passive of the verbs in parentheses. Check your accuracy. Then discuss with a partner: How do the two people feel about imported things? Who do you agree with more?**

ACCURACY CHECK

Do not use the base form of a verb after *be* with the passive. Use the past participle.

The coffee was ~~export~~ from Brazil. ✗

The coffee was exported from Brazil. ✓

back

I bought some roses this morning. The flower shop owner told me they [1] ____________ (grow) on a rose farm in Ecuador. After they [2] ____________ (cut), they [3] ____________ (store) in a refrigerated truck and [4] ____________ (take) to the airport. Then, after landing in Miami, they [5] ____________ (transport) by truck to her shop. Isn't that cool?

My coat [6] ____________ (make) in this city. It [7] ____________ (not, import). I like to support local companies. And because my coat [8] ____________ (produce) locally, it [9] ____________ (not, ship) across the world. That's important to me because a lot of resources, like gas, [10] ____________ (save).

C **Now go to page 138. Look at the grammar chart and do the grammar exercise for 10.2.**

FIND IT

D **Complete the sentences with simple past passive verbs and your own ideas. You can go online to get more ideas. Then share them with a partner.**

1 My phone ____________ .

2 Most of the food I eat ____________ .

3 A lot of the cars in my country ____________ .

4 SPEAKING

FIND IT

A GROUP WORK **Make a list together of five things you have with you. Guess what country they came from. You can go online to check where these types of things usually come from.**

OK, let's start with Carrie's bag. The company is American, so I guess it was made in the US.

Are you sure? Maybe it was designed in the US and made in India. Does it have a label?

B CLASS ACTIVITY **Share what you found out in exercise 4A with the class. Which things were made the furthest away? Were you surprised about where any of the things were made? Why? Which items were you not able to find out about?**

10.3 WHAT TO BUY?

LESSON OBJECTIVE
- question or approve of someone's choices

1 FUNCTIONAL LANGUAGE

sofa bed

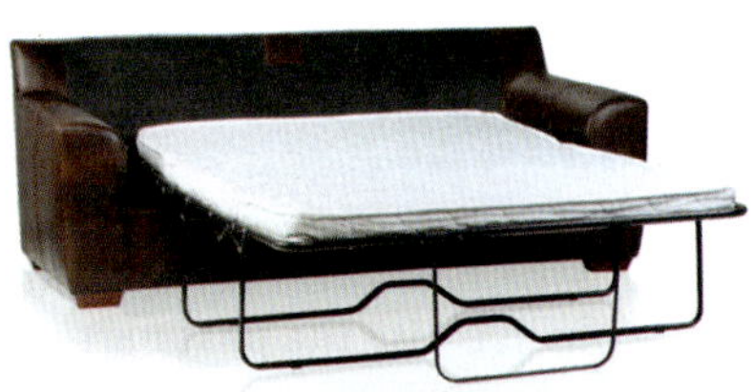

futon

air mattress

A 2.32 **Look at the pictures. Which one do you think is the most comfortable? Then read and listen. Which two things do Ryan and Andrea talk about? Which one will Ryan get?**

2.32 Audio script

A Hey, Andrea. Look at this picture. What do you think of this sofa bed? It's on sale.
B A sofa bed? **Why would you want to buy that**?
A My friend Faruk is visiting me from Istanbul. And I don't have a place for him to sleep.
B I see. But **do you really need a sofa bed**? You already have a couch.
A Yeah, but it's too small to sleep on. And Faruk will be here for a week. I want him to be comfortable. And after that, it'll be good for other friends who come to stay.
B True, but how often do people stay with you?
A Well, not very often, actually. You know, I could get an air mattress.
B **Now that's a good idea**. It's a lot cheaper, and you can just keep it in the closet when you aren't using it.
A OK, you convinced me. I'll get an air mattress.
B **That's what I would do**.

B **Complete the chart with expressions in bold from the conversation.**

Questioning someone's choices	Approving of someone's choices
1 ______ to buy/get that?	Now that's 3 ______.
2 ______ a sofa bed?	That's what 4 ______.
Are you sure you want to get that?	I think you made the right choice.

C 2.33 **Put the conversation in the correct order (1–4). Then listen and check.**

___ Yeah, but it's not great. I could borrow my sister's camera, I guess.
___ That's what I would do.
___ Are you sure you want to get that? Your phone has a camera, right?
___ I'm going to buy this new camera.

2 REAL-WORLD STRATEGY

A 2.34 **Darcy and Tara are shopping for gifts for their sister. Listen to their conversation. What does Tara want to buy? What does Darcy think about it?**

B 2.34 **Read the information in the box about changing your mind. Then listen again. What does Tara change her mind about? Why?**

> **CHANGING YOUR MIND**
>
> You can say *Now that I think about it* or *On second thought* when you change your mind.
>
> *OK, you convinced me. I'll get an air mattress.*
>
> *That's what I would do. But,* ***now that I think about it****, if you get the sofa bed, you could give me your couch!*

C **Complete the conversation with an expression from exercise 2B and a type of food. Then practice with a partner.**

A I'm going to have the black bean chili for lunch.
B Are you sure you want to get that? It's really spicy.
A [1] ______________________, I'll have [2] ______________.
B I think you made the right choice.

3 PRONUNCIATION: Saying /uː/, /ʊ/, and /aʊ/ vowel sounds

A 2.35 **Listen and repeat the different vowel sounds.**

/u/ you   /ʊ/ would   /aʊ/ couch

B 2.36 **Put the words in the correct categories. Then listen and check.**

could   Faruk   good
now   too   true

/u/	/ʊ/	/aʊ/

C **Practice the words from exercises 3A and 3B with a partner. Does your partner say the vowel sounds correctly?**

4 SPEAKING

A **Think of something you want to buy. Use one of the categories below or your own idea.**

clothing   food   furniture   sporting goods   technology

B PAIR WORK **Tell your partner what you want to buy. Your partner questions or approves of your choice. Take turns.**

I'm going to buy a bike helmet.

Do you really need a new helmet?

Yes, I do. Mine broke in two pieces!

C CLASS ACTIVITY **Tell the class what your partner wanted to buy and what you thought about it. Did your partner agree with your opinion?**

10.4 NOT JUST CUSTOMERS – FANS

LESSON OBJECTIVE

- write feedback about company products

Cacao beans are used to make Cocobar's products.

Jon is a fan of Cocobar's chocolate.

1 LISTENING

A PAIR WORK **Look at the pictures and read the captions. What's a fan? Talk about some companies that have a lot of fans.**

B 2.37 LISTEN FOR GIST **Listen to the podcast with host Rachel. What do business owners Erica and Tianyu say about their relationship with customers?**

C 2.37 IDENTIFY SPEAKERS **Listen again. Who gives this information? Write *R* for Rachel, *T* for Tianyu, or *E* for Erica. Sometimes more than one answer is possible. Then listen one more time and give answers for each item.**

1 ___ where the beans are from
2 ___ where the products are produced
3 ___ how they want customers to feel about the products
4 ___ why fans are important to the business
5 ___ the kind of feedback fans give

D PAIR WORK THINK CRITICALLY **What are some reasons why people might be fans of the company Cocobar? Think about one of your favorite companies. Why are you a fan?**

2 PRONUNCIATION: Listening for contrastive stress

A 2.38 **Listen to extracts from the podcast. Focus on the underlined words. Are they stressed more or less than the other words?**

1 I know your products are made from cacao beans that are imported from Peru, but they're produced locally with other natural ingredients.
2 We don't want them to just like our products – we want them to love our products.

B 2.39 **Listen. Underline two words in each sentence that receive the most stress.**

1 Some business owners care about customer reviews, but every business owner should.
2 I started making chocolate as a hobby, but it quickly became a business.
3 If our chocolate is a little more expensive, that's because it's also much higher quality.

C **Check (✓) the statement that is true.**

☐ We often place additional stress on words with similar ideas.
☐ We often place additional stress on words with different ideas.

3 WRITING

A **Read the feedback that fans posted on two company websites. What products do the fans give feedback about? Is the feedback positive, negative, or a little bit of both?**

Jon
36 posts

I ordered two boxes of Cocosations last week. The chocolate bars were delivered this morning, and my mom and I immediately tried them. They're fantastic! The caramel in the middle is not too sweet, and it goes well with the dark chocolate on the outside. We noticed a little salt was included in the caramel, and that's the magic touch. Salted caramel is very popular now. Although I usually buy Cocomax bars, I'll probably buy Cocosations from now on. This is another great product from my favorite candy company – thanks, Cocobar!

Adriana
4 posts

I'm a big fan of SUPERSPORT watches. I used to have a SUPERSPORT P1, but I lost it, so yesterday I went out and bought the new SUPERSPORT P2. I notice the screen of the new watch is made of glass. In the old model, the screen was made of hard plastic. I'm not sure glass is a good idea. It's true that the old plastic screen looked a little cheap. However, it was stronger than the glass screen, and that's very important for a sports watch. Otherwise, the P2 is really good and looks cool.

GLOSSARY

feedback *(n)* an opinion from someone about something that you have done or made

otherwise *(adv)* except for what you have just said; in other ways

B WRITING SKILLS **You can use *however* and *although* to contrast ideas. Read the sentences and underline the contrasting ideas in each sentence.**

1 Although I usually buy Cocomax bars, I'll probably buy Cocosations from now on.

2 It's true that the old plastic screen looked a little cheap. However, it was stronger than the glass screen.

REGISTER CHECK

***But* and *though* are informal ways to show contrasts in writing. *However* and *although* are often used in more formal writing.**

Informal

I used to have a SUPERSPORT P1, ***but*** *I lost it.*

I used to have a SUPERSPORT P1, ***though*** *I lost it.*

Formal

I used to have a SUPERSPORT P1. ***However,*** *I lost it.*

Although *I used to have a SUPERSPORT P1, I lost it.*

WRITE IT

C **Think of two products you're a fan of that are made by two different companies. Write feedback for each product. Describe the products and say what you like about them and what you don't like or how you think the companies can improve the products. Use *however* and *although* to contrast ideas.**

D PAIR WORK **Exchange feedback. What products did your partner write about? Are the posts positive, negative, or a mixture of both?**

10.5 TIME TO SPEAK
Shopping psychology

LESSON OBJECTIVE
- design a commercial

Seven Reasons Why We Buy

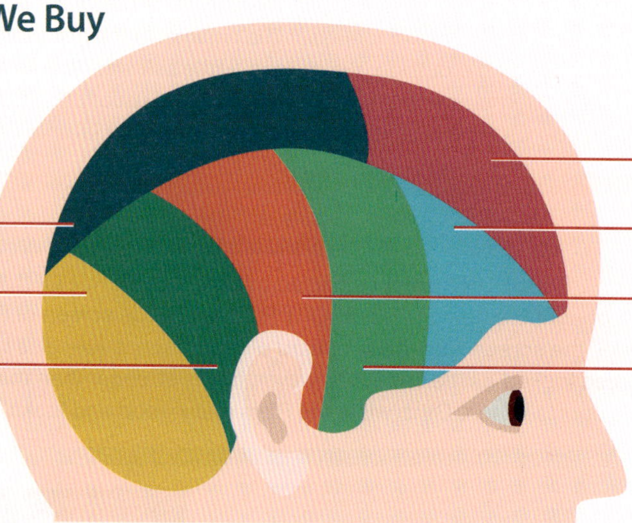

A DISCUSS Look at the picture of the seven reasons why we buy. In groups, think of some examples of things that are bought for each reason.

B DISCUSS People often buy things for more than one reason. Look at the things in the box. What are some reasons people buy these things?

fast food   phone/internet plans   toothpaste

FIND IT

C RESEARCH Talk about commercials you've seen for the things in part B. You can go online to watch some commercials. Which reasons for buying do the commercials make you think about? Are they the same as the reasons you discussed in part B?

D PREPARE Imagine you work for an advertising company. With your group, choose a product that is used by most people. Think about reasons why people might want to buy it. Then, as a group, think of an idea for a commercial for the product.

E PRESENT Describe your commercial to the class.

F AGREE The class chooses the best commercial.

To check your progress, go to page 156.

USEFUL PHRASES

DISCUSS
… are bought for / because / in order to …

RESEARCH / PREPARE
You see a (person/ thing). They (do something).
And then … At the end, …

UNIT OBJECTIVES

- talk about how to succeed
- talk about imaginary situations
- give opinions and ask for agreement
- write a personal story
- talk about a person you admire

PUSHING YOURSELF

11

START SPEAKING

A Where do you think this woman is? Why do you think she's there? What challenges do you think she's dealing with?

B Talk about something you did that was challenging. How did you feel before you did it? while you did it? after you did it?

C Why do you think people push themselves to do difficult things? For ideas, watch Andrea's video.

REAL STUDENT

Do you agree with Andrea?

11.1 SECRETS OF SUCCESS

LESSON OBJECTIVE
- talk about how to succeed

1 LANGUAGE IN CONTEXT

A **Read the article by Ross Rivera. What is *failure*? Does Ross think it is a good or bad thing? Why?**

B **Read again. What qualities does the article say are good for employees to have?**

DO I NEED TO *fail* MORE?

As a technology writer, I spend lots of time making sure each article is as good as my last one. I've had a lot of success in my career. But could this be a bad thing?

I write about a lot of tech companies that fail, but people in the industry actually see failure as normal and an important part of later success. Evan Williams and Noah Glass, for example, once **set up** a podcasting company that didn't **work out**. They **got over it** – and joined some friends to start Twitter. A lot of international companies also agree that you have to **work at** success. Managers often promote employees who **keep up** the hard work and don't **give up** during bad times. That really makes someone **stand out** from the crowd.

I've been thinking about how I can fail more, and I think I **figured it out.** I like my writing job and don't want to **give it up**, so I'm moving on … to writing music reviews! And if that doesn't work out … well, I just hope failure is good for me.

– Ross Rivera

Evan Williams

C PAIR WORK **Do you think the change Ross is going to make is a good idea? Why or why not?**

INSIDER ENGLISH

We say *I'm moving on* to mean *I'm starting something new* or *I'm ready for something new.*

2 VOCABULARY: Succeeding

A 2.40 **Find the expressions in the text and complete them with the correct preposition. Then listen and check.**

1 set ________
2 work ________
3 get ________ something
4 work ________ something
5 keep ________
6 give ________
7 stand ________
8 figure something ________
9 give something ________

B **Now go to page 151. Do the vocabulary exercises for 11.1.**

C PAIR WORK **Which of these statements do you agree with the most? Why?**

1 If your job is making you unhappy, give it up, and set up your own business.
2 It's good to stand out and not be like everyone else.
3 If you want to be successful, never give up – keep up the hard work, no matter what.
4 If something goes wrong, don't get upset – get over it.

I don't think it's a good idea to give up your job. You can do something fun on weekends instead.

3 GRAMMAR: Phrasal verbs

A **Circle the correct answers. Use the sentences in the grammar box to help you.**

1 **All** / **Some** phrasal verbs have an object.
2 We can **always** / **sometimes** put the object after the two words of a phrasal verb.
3 We can **always** / **sometimes** put the object between the two words of a phrasal verb.

Phrasal verbs

If that doesn't **work out**, I hope failure is good for me.
They **set up** a company. They **set** it **up**.
I **figured out** the answer. I **figured** it **out**.
I don't want to **give up** my job. I don't want to **give** it **up**.
They **got over** the failure. They **got over** it.

! ***Give up*** **can have an object or it can have no object.**
You have a good job. Don't ***give*** *it* ***up****.*
Keep trying. Don't ***give up****.*

B **Now go to page 139. Look at the grammar chart and do the grammar exercise for 11.1.**

C PAIR WORK **Rewrite each sentence using *it*. Compare with your partner. Then discuss who might say these things (your boss? teacher? friend?).**

1 You should **set up** a new company.
You should set it up.
2 You can **figure out** the solution.
3 We're **working at** the solution.
4 Don't **give up** your job.
5 You'll **get over** the disappointment.
6 **Keep up** the good work.

D **Complete the sentences with your own ideas. Then share them with a partner.**

1 I'll never give up …
2 I'd like to figure out …
3 If you want to stand out, you can …

4 SPEAKING

A **Think of a time in the past when something didn't go well for you, a friend, or a family member. It can be true or you can make it up. What effects did the failure have? Were any of the effects positive? Take notes.**

B GROUP WORK **Share your ideas with the group. What happened after the failures? Did any of the failures lead to successes?**

11.2 NOW THAT'S INTERESTING!

LESSON OBJECTIVE
- talk about imaginary situations

1 LANGUAGE IN CONTEXT

A **Look at the picture. What do you know about crocodiles? How dangerous are they? Why?**

B 2.41 **Read and listen to an interview with a successful businesswoman. What unusual and surprising question does Miles ask?**

C 2.41 PAIR WORK **Read and listen again. How does Selma decide what she would do? Why does she use that approach?**

2.41 Audio script

Miles So, let's get right to it. Why do you think you've been so successful? Is it because you've taken risks?

Selma I think that's a big part of it – yes.

Miles Would you risk *everything* for money and success? Even your life?

Selma My life? In what kind of situation?

Miles Well, … would you swim across a river full of crocodiles if I offered you a million dollars?

Selma Now that's interesting! Let's see … if I succeeded, the reward would be fantastic. That much money would have a big effect on my life. But I'd have to consider the risk carefully – and think about how to reduce it. So, I'd find out about the number of crocodiles in the river. Um … I'd research ways to protect myself. If I spent $100,000 on a "crocodile-proof" suit, I'd still make $900,000!

Miles You're really thinking about this *seriously* …

Selma In business, you have to consider all of the options – compare the advantages and disadvantages – and then decide if the risk is worth it.

Miles And if your research showed the risk was high?

Selma I wouldn't do it. I wouldn't be able to spend a million dollars if I ended up inside a crocodile!

2 VOCABULARY: Opportunities and risks

FIND IT

A 2.42 **Listen and repeat the words. Which words are nouns? verbs? both nouns and verbs? You can use a dictionary or your phone to help you. Then find and underline nine of the words in the conversation in exercise 1B.**

advantage	consider	disadvantage	effect	goal	option
purpose	research	result	reward	risk	situation

B **Now go to page 151. Do the vocabulary exercises for 11.2.**

C GROUP WORK **Are you a risk-taker? What risks do you take? Which ones do you avoid? Why? For ideas, watch Angie's video.**

Is Angie a risk-taker?

3 GRAMMAR: Present and future unreal conditionals

A **Circle the correct answers. Use the sentences in the grammar box to help you.**

1 In the *if* clause, use ***would* + verb / the simple past** to describe an imagined situation.
2 In the main clause, use ***would* + verb / the simple past** to describe a predicted result.

Present and future unreal conditionals

Would you **swim** across a river full of crocodiles **if** I **offered** you a million dollars?
If I **succeeded**, the reward **would be** fantastic.
If I **spent** $100,000 on a "crocodile-proof" suit, **I'd** still **make** $900,000!
I **wouldn't be** able to spend a million dollars **if** I **ended up** inside a crocodile!

B **Now go to page 139. Look at the grammar chart and do the grammar exercise for 11.2.**

C **Complete the sentences with your own ideas. Check your accuracy. Then share your answers with a partner.**

1 If I had to run a marathon, I ______________________ .
2 I would save money if I ______________________ .
3 I ______________________ if I had to give up one thing.
4 If my friends ______________________ , I would be excited.
5 If I were really strong, I ______________________ .
6 My parents would be happy if ______________________ .

ACCURACY CHECK

Do not use *would* in the *if* clause. Use the simple past.

If the risk ~~would be~~ high, I wouldn't do it. ✗
If the risk were high, I wouldn't do it. ✓

D PAIR WORK **Ask and answer the questions.**

1 Which sport would you choose if you wanted to play a new one?
2 If you started a new business, what would it be?
3 Where would you fly if you owned a plane?

4 SPEAKING

A **Think of three different activities to complete the question below. They can be silly, serious, easy, or extreme. Be creative! Take notes.**

Would you … if I offered you a million dollars?

B PAIR WORK **Compare your activities. Choose your two favorite "Would you …" questions.**

C GROUP WORK **Work with another pair. Ask and answer your questions from exercise 4A. Say what you would need to know before deciding.**

Would you walk on a tightrope if I offered you a million dollars?

I think I would. First, I'd find out …

11.3 IT'S NOT WORTH IT

LESSON OBJECTIVE
- give opinions and ask for agreement

1 FUNCTIONAL LANGUAGE

A 2.43 **Look at the photo of the man. How does he feel, and why? Then read and listen to two people talking about him. What are his problems? What do his friends think he should do?**

2.43 Audio script

A Milo just texted me again from his office. He's really unhappy with work.
B I know. But I guess it's hard to give up a good job.
A **Yeah, especially when** it pays so well. But he has to work long hours, he's stressed, and he can't stop thinking about work, even on the weekends.
B That's not good.
A And he's a hard worker. He really pushes himself. But he thinks he's getting nowhere. If I had his job, I'd leave. **Don't you think**?
B **Yeah, I agree with you**. It's not worth it.
A But I wouldn't leave right away. I'd find a new job before I left.
B Hmm, not me. I wouldn't stay at a job if I didn't like it. And I wouldn't go out and get another job immediately. It would be a chance to start something new, **right**? I mean, Milo doesn't like his job, so maybe he should think about a new career.
A **Good point**. He needs to find something he likes.

B **Complete the chart with expressions in bold from the conversation.**

Asking for agreement	Agreeing
Don't you [1] ______ ?	[3] ______ it pays so well.
… , [2] ______ ?	Yeah, I [4] ______ with you.
… , you know?	Good [5] ______ .
Don't you agree?	I see what you mean.

C 2.44 **Put the conversation in the correct order (1–4). Then listen and check.**

___ Good point. I should call them today, right?
___ I applied for that job two weeks ago, but I haven't heard from the company yet.
___ I would. You need to show them you're really serious about the job.
___ I think you should call them. Then they'll know you're interested. Don't you agree?

2 REAL-WORLD STRATEGY

A 2.45 **Listen to a conversation between Noah and Callie, two of Milo's colleagues. What did they both notice?**

B 2.45 **Read the information in the box about softening an opinion. Then listen again. Which opinions do Noah and Callie soften?**

SOFTENING AN OPINION

You can use *I guess* or *I feel like* to soften an opinion.

***I guess** it's hard to give up a good job. /* ***I feel like** it's hard to give up a good job.*

C **Complete another conversation with expressions from exercise 2B. More than one answer is possible. Then practice with a partner.**

A That exam was really strange. ________________ there were some errors in the questions.

B Yeah, I see what you mean. ________________ we should ask the teacher about it. Don't you agree?

3 PRONUNCIATION: Saying /ʃ/ and /ʤ/ sounds

A 2.46 **Listen and repeat. Focus on the sounds of the letters in bold.**

1 /ʃ/ pu**sh**es He really pu**sh**es himself. 2 /ʤ/ **j**ust Milo **j**ust texted me.

B 2.47 **Which words have the /ʃ/ sound, and which have the /ʤ/ sound? Put the words in the correct categories. Then listen and check.**

especially job should
fashion eject

/ʃ/	/ʤ/

C PAIR WORK **Practice saying the words in exercises 3A and 3B with a partner. Does your partner say the /ʃ/ and /ʤ/ sounds correctly?**

4 SPEAKING

A PAIR WORK **Together, choose one of these topics to discuss. Choose opposite sides of the argument.**

1 Technology is driving people apart. **vs.** Technology is bringing people together.
2 Get a degree or certificate before getting a job. **vs.** You don't need a degree. Get a job and learn while you work.
3 Pets are good for people. **vs.** Pets are a lot of trouble.

B **On your own, think about opinions and points that support your side of the argument in exercise 4A. Take notes.**

C PAIR WORK **Give your opinions. Try to get your partner to agree. You can use expressions to soften some of your opinions. When you're finished, tell the class which topic you chose and whether you agreed in the end.**

Technology is definitely driving people apart. Everyone just looks at their screens all the time. No one talks anymore.

True, but they're still communicating.

11.4 OUTSIDE THE COMFORT ZONE

LESSON OBJECTIVE
- write a personal story

1 READING

A IDENTIFY POINT OF VIEW **Read the article. Then read about point of view (POV) below. Which POV does the writer use? Why do you think she uses it?**

- ☐ First person: The writer talks about herself and her own experiences.
- ☐ Second person: The writer speaks directly to the reader.
- ☐ Third person: The writer talks about other people's experiences.

B NOTE TAKING **Read the article again. What is your "comfort zone"? Is it good or bad? Why? How does the article suggest "leaving your comfort zone"? Take notes. Then compare your notes with a partner.**

SEARCH

LEAVING YOUR COMFORT ZONE

Maybe you've had the same job for several years. Or maybe you do the same things for fun over and over again. You're in your "comfort zone." On the one hand, you feel safe, successful, and … comfortable. On the other hand, you aren't challenging yourself, and your life is pretty boring. Is it worth it to change?

Research shows there are a lot of advantages to doing new activities outside of your routine. Challenges help you think in new ways and learn new things about yourself. And they help you see that one bad event isn't the end of the world.

Don't worry – you don't have to begin by running a marathon! Start small. How about going to a new restaurant? At the gym, you might try a class you've never taken before. If you're into hip-hop, try listening to EDM or classical music! These are all small changes, but the benefits are huge.

So the next time you're ordering your favorite coffee, think about choosing something different. You might hate it … or you might discover your new favorite drink!

GLOSSARY
benefit *(n)* something that helps you

C PAIR WORK **What is your comfort zone? Are you doing things that are outside that comfort zone? How does it make you feel?**

D THINK CRITICALLY **How far is "too far" to push yourself out of your comfort zone? Is there a risk to changing things in your life?**

A **Look at the pictures and read Marty's story. What was his fear? How did he overcome it?**

Conquering a fear

I have a surprising secret: I used to be really frightened of escalators. Yes, escalators: those moving stairs you see everywhere. It's actually a very common fear. For years, if I saw an escalator, I would do anything to avoid it. If I did get on, my heart would beat really fast. My friends told me that very few people fall off escalators. "I know," I'd say, "but I don't want to be that one!"

Then one day I thought, "Enough! I'm going to deal with this now." I decided to start with a short escalator and then try the longer ones. At first, it wasn't too bad. The hardest part was facing an escalator in a subway station that went deep underground. That first step was awful! I was sure I was going to fall, but I held on and didn't give up. And the more I practiced, the easier it got. Now I ride those moving stairs with confidence!

I learned something useful from this. On the one hand, it's good to push yourself out of your comfort zone. On the other hand, you don't want to push yourself too far, too fast. Take it slow! You might surprise yourself.

B **WRITING SKILLS Read about comparing facts and ideas. Then underline the two opposite ways of thinking in Marty's story.**

We use *On the one hand, …* and *On the other hand, …* to compare two different facts or two opposite ways of thinking about a situation.

On the one hand, I was afraid to ride escalators. On the other hand, I was tired of being afraid.

WRITE IT

C **Write a story about a time when you pushed yourself out of your comfort zone. It can be true, or you can make it up. Use *on the one hand* and *on the other hand* to compare facts or ideas. Give advice to the reader.**

D **PAIR WORK Exchange stories. Would your partner's advice work for you?**

REGISTER CHECK

First-person stories often contain a lot of personal details and feelings. Articles in the third person often contain more facts and neutral information. Notice the differences between a sentence in Marty's story and a sentence that could be in an article about Marty.

My friends told me that very few people fall off escalators.

According to the National Institutes of Health, there are only 10,000 escalator injuries per year in the US that result in emergency room visits.

11.5 TIME TO SPEAK

Success stories

LESSON OBJECTIVE

- talk about a person you admire

A **DISCUSS** Look at the pictures. What do you know about these people? What areas have they been successful in? Tell a partner.

FIND IT

B **RESEARCH** Look at the categories of successful people below. In groups, make a list with one successful person from each category. You can go online for ideas. What were some of the challenges these people faced? What did they do to succeed?

athletes | businesspeople | entertainers | politicians | scientists

C **DISCUSS** Imagine these people are going to help you achieve success in different parts of your life. Who would you want to:

- teach your class?
- help you do something you're afraid to try?
- show you how they do their job?
- teach you a new skill?
- give you advice about money?

D **DECIDE** Look at the magazine. Who would you put on the cover? Choose the person your group admires most from part C.

E **PRESENT** Share your choice with the class. Explain what skills or knowledge this person can offer and how their struggle for success helped them. Answer any questions about the person.

F **AGREE** As a class, choose the best person for the cover.

To check your progress, go to page 156.

USEFUL PHRASES

DISCUSS

I know him/her! He/She is …

I would want … to … because …

That would be …

DECIDE

I'd put … on the cover because …

… is a good choice because …

I wouldn't choose … because …

PRESENT

We chose … because …

We felt that …

We admire … for his/her …

UNIT OBJECTIVES

- talk about accidents
- talk about extreme experiences
- describe and ask about feelings
- write an anecdote about a life lesson
- plan a fun learning experience

LIFE'S LITTLE LESSONS

12

START SPEAKING

A **Look at the picture. What do you think is happening?**

B **What might have happened in the five minutes before this accident? Make up a story.**

C **Who do you think learned a lesson in this picture? What lessons do you think he or she learned? For ideas, watch Andrea's video.**

REAL STUDENT

Does Andrea think the same thing as you?

12.1 IT WAS AN ACCIDENT!

LESSON OBJECTIVE
- talk about accidents

1 LANGUAGE IN CONTEXT

A 2.48 **Look at the picture. What do you talk about at mealtimes? Then read and listen to Lorena, Talya, and Mark's conversation. What do their stories have in common?**

2.48 Audio script

Lorena When I was a kid, I picked up the ketchup bottle from the dinner table and started shaking it to mix it up. The lid came off, and ketchup spilled everywhere! You've never seen anything like it! Everyone was mad at me. I felt bad about it, but it was also funny. Anyway, it was an accident!

Talya I know what you mean. One time, I was in a restaurant somewhere with my parents. My dad was cutting his steak, and suddenly his knife slipped, and his peas flew everywhere. He was so embarrassed, but my mom said, "It's not what happens – it's how you deal with it." So we laughed, got up from the table, and quickly picked up all of the peas.

Mark That reminds me … I was eating in a restaurant once, and I knocked something off my plate. I looked on the floor but couldn't see anything. Then the woman at the next table reached into her open purse on the floor and pulled out a chicken leg! She said nothing. She didn't blame me – she just gave me the chicken leg. I'm sure she never left her purse open in a restaurant again!

B 2.48 **Read and listen again. Answer the questions.**

1 What feelings did Lorena have about her ketchup accident?
2 What lesson did Talya learn from her father's accident?
3 Where did Mark's chicken leg go?

INSIDER ENGLISH

We use *You've never seen anything like it* to mean that something was incredible or very unusual.

2 VOCABULARY: Describing accidents

A 2.49 PAIR WORK **Listen and repeat the verbs. Which verbs are actions and which are feelings? Then find and underline ten of these verbs in the conversation in exercise 1A.**

be mad at	blame	damage	destroy	fall out
feel bad (about)	knock off	leave on	leave open	pick up
pull out	shake	slip	spill	

B **Now go to page 152. Do the vocabulary exercises for 12.1.**

C PAIR WORK **Describe an accident you had or saw during a meal, and say how people reacted. For ideas, watch Celeste's video.**

What accident did Celeste see?

3 GRAMMAR: Indefinite pronouns

A **Circle the correct answers. Use the sentences in the grammar box to help you.**

1 Indefinite pronouns with *every-* describe **some** / **all** members of a group.

2 Indefinite pronouns with ***some-*** / ***any-*** are usually used in questions and negative sentences.

3 Indefinite pronouns with *no-* mean "**only one**" / "**none**."

Indefinite pronouns

Ketchup spilled **everywhere**.	I was in a restaurant **somewhere**.
Everyone was mad at me.	You've never seen **anything** like it!
I knocked **something** off my plate.	She said **nothing**.

B **Now go to page 140. Look at the grammar chart and do the grammar exercise for 12.1.**

C PAIR WORK **Complete the sentences with indefinite pronouns. Check your accuracy. Then say if the sentences are true for you or if you agree.**

1 I didn't have ______ for breakfast this morning.

2 ______ once borrowed my headphones and damaged them.

3 ______ ever leaves their windows open at night here. It's too cold.

4 I spilled ______ on my clothes earlier today.

5 ______ has accidents, but they shouldn't feel bad about them.

6 I once lost my keys. They fell out of my pocket ______ .

ACCURACY CHECK

Be careful with the spelling of *no one*. It is not one word like the other indefinite pronouns.

~~Noone~~ saw me spill my drink. ✗

No one saw me spill my drink. ✓

D **Complete the sentences with your own ideas. Then share with a partner.**

1 I damaged ______ by accident, but nobody ______ .

2 I looked everywhere for ______ , but ______ .

3 Once, I spilled ______ at someone's house. Everybody ______ .

4 SPEAKING

A **Think about a time when you had a small or amusing accident. What happened? How did you feel? What did you learn from the accident? Take notes.**

B GROUP WORK **Describe your accident and say what you learned. Listen to the other stories and ask questions to find out more. Whose accident was the funniest? Who learned the most valuable lesson?**

I got a new phone a few weeks ago, but I didn't buy a case for it right away. I was walking home when I dropped my phone on the sidewalk.

Oh, no! Was there glass everywhere?

Yeah, there was. Luckily, someone lent me their phone for the day. I learned my lesson: get a case for your phone.

12.2 LEARNING UNDERWATER

LESSON OBJECTIVE
- talk about extreme experiences

1 LANGUAGE IN CONTEXT

A **Look at the picture. Would you like to do this? Why or why not?**

B **Read Bryce's social media post. How long has he been taking his diving course? What has he learned?**

C **Read the post again. Which two things made Bryce feel good today?**

Profile | **Wall** | **Friends**

I'm exhausted … but day two of my diving course was terrific! Last night, I said that I was feeling miserable after a difficult start. But today, I'm thrilled. Elena (my instructor) told me that I had done really well. She said that I was concentrating on my dives, and that had made a huge difference because I'd stayed calm today.

I definitely didn't feel calm this morning when Elena told us we were going to learn to deal with air problems. Then she said we would be at a depth of 45 feet (15 meters), so we couldn't swim to the surface quickly. She said we would have to work as a team and share air. We practiced a few times just below the surface of the water. And then we went down deep. I was terrified. But in the end, everything was fine. And while we were down there, hundreds of tiny fish swam past us. It was a magnificent sight. Suddenly, I realized I was enjoying myself.

So, the five things I've learned about diving are: concentrate, stay calm, work as a team, practice, and enjoy it. That's good advice for whatever you're doing, I guess.

2 VOCABULARY: Describing extremes

A 2.50 **Find and underline eight of the words in the post in exercise 1B. Then match all of the words to the synonyms. One item has two words that mean the same. Listen and check.**

boiling	enormous	exhausted	freezing	huge	magnificent
miserable	starving	terrific	terrified	thrilled	tiny

1 ________ very beautiful or good
2 ________ , ________ very big
3 ________ very cold
4 ________ very good
5 ________ very happy
6 ________ very hot
7 ________ very hungry
8 ________ very sad
9 ________ very scared
10 ________ very small
11 ________ very tired

B **Now go to page 152. Do the vocabulary exercises for 12.2.**

FIND IT

C PAIR WORK **Think of a surprising situation you have heard about recently. You can go online to read recent news stories. Describe it with extreme adjectives.**

Did you know four hikers got lost on Mount Elbrus last year? Fortunately, they were rescued!

They must have been miserable! Were they freezing?

3 GRAMMAR: Reported speech

A **How do these words change in reported speech? Write them below. Use the sentences in the grammar box to help you.**

is / are → ________ / ________ *can* → ________

will → ________ *did* → ________ *have done* → ________

Reported speech

Direct speech	**Reported speech**
"It**'s** difficult."	She said (that) it **was** difficult.
"They**'re** doing well."	She said (that) they **were** doing well.
"They **did** well."	She said (that) they **had done** well.
"They**'ve done** well."	She said (that) they **had done** well.
"They **can** do it."	She said (that) they **could** do it.
"It **will** be difficult."	She said (that) it **would** be difficult.
"It**'s going to** be easy."	She said (that) it **was going to** be easy.

B PAIR WORK **Change the comments to reported speech. Then cover the sentences on the right and practice with a partner. You say a sentence on the left, and your partner says, "He/She said … " Take turns.**

1 "We can't have a break." She said that we ________.
2 "We're going to start early." She told us we ________.
3 "It will be a long day." She said it ________.
4 "You took too many risks." She told me that I ________.
5 "It's an important rule." She said it ________.
6 "You've worked hard." She told us that we ________.

C **Now go to page 140. Look at the grammar chart and do the grammar exercise for 12.2.**

4 SPEAKING

A PAIR WORK **Think of an extreme experience you had. Use one of the ideas below or your own ideas. Tell your partner about your experience and say how you felt. Change roles.**

a challenging activity a fun day out a long trip
extreme or unusual weather an amazing place

B PAIR WORK **Work with a different partner. Tell him or her about your last partner's experience.**

David went rock climbing last week. He said that he had never tried it before. He said that he had been terrified, but he would do it again.

C PAIR WORK **Go to the person your partner talked about. Tell him or her what your partner said about him or her. Did your partner get all the details correct?**

12.3 A HOTEL NIGHTMARE

LESSON OBJECTIVE

- describe and ask about feelings

1 FUNCTIONAL LANGUAGE

A **2.51 Look at the picture. What do you think is happening? How do you think the people feel? Then read and listen. What was the problem? How was it solved?**

2.51 Audio script

A So, what happened to you last weekend? I got your text. You said you were at a hotel on the coast, or somewhere, and you were having problems …

B Yeah, one big problem! I reserved a room online with a hotel-booking website, not directly with the hotel. And when I got to the hotel, there was no reservation!

A Oh, no! **You must have been furious.**

B **Actually, I was shocked.** Then I was mad at myself for not checking with the hotel before I got there.

A So, what happened?

B Well, first they said I should call the booking company. But then they checked the computer and told me there were no rooms available anyway. **What a nightmare!**

A Yeah. What did you do?

B I called the booking company and told them about the problem. They apologized and said they'd find me another hotel while I waited. Then they told me they had a room – in a five-star hotel! And I didn't have to pay anything more.

A **I bet that made you feel good.**

B Yeah. **I couldn't stop smiling.** It turned into a dream vacation!

B **Complete the chart with expressions in bold from the conversation.**

Describing your feelings	Asking about or guessing others' feelings
1 ______	4 ______
2 ______	5 ______
3 ______	I bet that made you feel bad.
It was a horrible/fantastic experience.	How did that make you feel?

C PAIR WORK **Circle the correct response. Then practice with a partner.**

1 **A** I finally passed my driver's test.
B **a** How did that make you feel? **b** I bet that made you feel bad.

2 **A** You must have been excited about the news.
B **a** What a nightmare! **b** Actually, I was shocked.

3 **A** The airline lost my bags.
B **a** It was a horrible experience. **b** You must have been furious.

4 **A** How did you feel after the exam?
B **a** I bet that made you feel good. **b** Great! I couldn't stop smiling.

2 REAL-WORLD STRATEGY

A 2.52 **Listen to Jimmy telling Mi-young about a presentation. Why did it start late? How did that make Jimmy feel?**

B 2.52 **Read the information in the box about ending a story. Then listen again. What expression does Jimmy use to end his story? How did his story end?**

> **ENDING A STORY**
>
> You can use *In the end* or *After all that* to end a story. The expressions often show there were some problems before the situation ended.
>
> *Yeah. I couldn't stop smiling.* ***After all that****, it turned into a dream vacation!*

C PAIR WORK **Tell your partner about a time when you had some problems, but things ended in a good way. Use one of the expressions from the box to end your story. Take turns.**

D PAIR WORK **Student A: Go to page 157. Student B: Go to page 158. Follow the instructions.**

3 PRONUNCIATION: Saying *-ed* at the end of a word

A 2.53 **Listen. Focus on the sound of the *-ed* at the end of each word in bold.**

/id/ waited   /t/ shocked   /d/ happened

B 2.54 **Match the words below with the correct sound for their *-ed* endings. Then listen and check.**

called	checked	decided
exhausted	knocked	looked
passed	reserved	

/id/	/t/	/d/

C **Practice the conversation with a partner. Does your partner say the *-ed* endings correctly?**

A What a day. I'm exhausted.

B Why what happened?

A You know that project I've been working on? Well my boss decided that we needed to do the whole thing over. And the thing is he waited until we were almost done to tell us!

B What a nightmare! I hope he apologized at least.

4 SPEAKING

A **Choose one of these expressions and think of an experience that goes with it. Use a personal experience or make one up. Include your feelings about what happened. Take notes.**

- What a nightmare!
- What an exhausting day!
- What a great experience!
- What a fantastic trip!

B PAIR WORK **Tell your partner about your experience. Your partner asks about or guesses how you felt. Change roles and repeat.**

My friend and I were hiking last weekend, and we got lost.

Oh, no! Weren't you scared?

12.4 LESSONS LEARNED?

LESSON OBJECTIVE
- write an anecdote about a life lesson

1 LISTENING

A PREDICT **You are going to hear Tasha Roberts give a talk. Look at the pictures. What do you think she's going to talk about?**

B 2.55 LISTEN FOR MAIN IDEAS **Listen to the talk. Were your ideas in exercise 1A correct? What other example does Tasha give? What's the main point she illustrates with these examples?**

C 2.55 LISTEN FOR DEFINITIONS **Listen again. Tasha defines some words in her talk. Complete the definitions as you listen. You will need to change the form of some of the words.**

1 *Constantly* means something happens ______________ .
2 *Temporarily* means something happens ______________ .
3 A *creature of habit* is someone who ______________ .
4 An *intention* is something that you ______________ .

D PAIR WORK THINK CRITICALLY **Which statement below do you think Tasha would agree with? Why? Which one do you agree with?**

You can easily learn from your mistakes.
You can learn from your mistakes, but it's difficult.
You can't learn from your mistakes.

2 PRONUNCIATION: Listening for *'ll*

A 2.56 **Listen. Focus on the difference in the uncontracted and contracted forms.**

You will be able to stop telling that same bad joke!
You'll be able to stop telling that same bad joke!

B 2.57 **Listen. Focus on the words in bold. Circle the vowel sound you hear.**

1 /uː/ /ʊ/ **You'll** know how to make little lessons turn into life lessons.
2 /iː/ /ɪ/ **We'll** soon go back to our old habits.
3 /eɪ/ /e/ **They'll** learn from this experience.

C **Circle the correct word to complete the statement.**

When the *'ll* comes after a vowel sound, that vowel sound is often *shortened / lengthened*.

3 WRITING

A **Read Gavin's anecdote. What wrong lesson did he learn? What did he learn in the end?**

When I was ten, my teacher told me I had to write a report about volcanoes and make a model volcano. I delayed working on the project until the day before my presentation, and then I told my parents after dinner. At first, they were mad at me, and I felt really bad, but then they said they'd help me. We researched volcanoes online and went to a craft store just before it closed to buy things to make the volcano. We worked on it until midnight, and I wrote the report. The next day, I gave a terrific talk. All of my classmates said I had made a cool volcano, and the teacher took a picture of me with it.

This taught me that I could wait until the last minute and still do a magnificent job. But it was the wrong lesson to learn, and I spent the next ten years trying to unlearn it. In high school and college, everything was harder, but because of my volcano, I told myself I could wait until the last minute. I failed a lot before I learned how to manage my time well. I think now that it would have been better if my parents had let me fail when I was ten. I would have learned a valuable lesson a lot earlier.

B **WRITING SKILLS Read about using expressions with similar meanings. Then find expressions in exercise 3A that have similar meanings to 1–5 and write them in the correct place.**

We often use different expressions with similar meanings to make our writing more interesting and to avoid repeating the same words.

1 This taught me = I learned
2 delay = ______
3 until the day before X = ______
4 terrific = ______
5 presentation = ______

REGISTER CHECK

In writing anecdotes, we often use longer sentences with conjunctions. It is similar to how we speak when we tell someone a story.

***At first**, they were mad at me, **and** I felt really bad, **but** then they said they'd help me.*

WRITE IT

C **Write an anecdote about an important lesson you learned. Think of a time when you changed your behavior based on something that happened in the past. Write at least two paragraphs. Use different expressions with similar meanings to avoid repeating the same words.**

D **PAIR WORK Exchange stories. Talk about the lessons you learned. Have you learned the same lesson? How would you change your behavior based on your partner's lesson?**

The lesson you learned is such a good one. Managing your money is important. I would like to be better at that!

I know what you mean! I liked your lesson about being nice to servers in restaurants. I learned that, too, when …

12.5 TIME TO SPEAK
Skillful fun

LESSON OBJECTIVE
- plan a fun learning experience

paddle-boarding

go-karting

karaoke

bowling

FIND IT

A **RESEARCH** With a partner, talk about fun activities you've done where you learned or practiced some skills. Look at the pictures to help you think of ideas. You can go online to learn the names in English of activities you like. Then choose the activity you've done that you enjoyed the most.

B **DISCUSS** Move around the class and tell others about the activity you chose in part A. Explain why it was fun, and try to persuade them that they'll enjoy it, too. Listen to what others say about their activities.

C **DECIDE** Work in groups. Tell the group about an activity you heard about in part B (not your own activity) that sounded fun. Say what the person told you about it. The group chooses the best activity.

D **PRESENT** Tell the class about the activity your group chose in part C. Try to persuade your classmates that they'll enjoy it.

E **AGREE** Imagine the class is going to do one of the activities from part D together. Choose something that would be good for everyone. Avoid anything that anyone would be scared to do.

To check your progress, go to page 156.

USEFUL PHRASES

PREPARE
Once, I went/did/tried …
It was terrific!
At first, I was terrified, but then …

DECIDE
… told me that …
He/She said that …
I think it sounds fun.
I'd like to try it.

AGREE
Nobody else wants to …
… said he/she was terrified of …
Most of us would like to …

REVIEW 4 (UNITS 10–12)

1 VOCABULARY

A Which word or phrase doesn't belong in each set? Circle it.

1 **Materials:**	cotton	glass	plastic	polyester	ship
2 **Describing materials:**	artificial	light	option	soft	strong
3 **Production:**	design	freezing	grow	pick	produce
4 **Distribution:**	deliver	export	knock off	transport	store
5 **Opportunities:**	advantage	goal	purpose	reward	warm
6 **Accidents:**	blame	damage	destroy	leather	spill
7 **Extremes:**	huge	manufacture	starving	terrific	tiny

B **Look at the words you circled in exercise 1A. Add them to the correct set.**

C **Add two more words or phrases that you know to each category.**

2 GRAMMAR

A **Complete the paragraph with the correct form of the verbs in parentheses ( ).**

"The planet will get hotter in the next 100 years," said many scientists in 2017. In fact, they said that the planet [1] ________ (become) 3°C hotter before 2100. That is a major problem, and what we consume has a huge impact. Everyone [2] ________ (be) worried about the planet, but no one [3] ________ (know) how to solve the problem. We often consume fruits and vegetables that [4] ________ (produce) in other parts of the country. Those items [5] ________ (transport) by trucks or planes, and that increases pollution. If everyone [6] ________ (buy) their food from local farmers, the world [7] ________ (be) less polluted. Another problem is the use of chemicals. In the past, not so many chemicals [8] ________ (use) by farmers. Certainly, people [9] ________ (consume) more organic food if it [10] ________ (not be) so expensive.

B PAIR WORK **What did you have for breakfast this morning? Where do you think those food items were produced? How far do you think they were transported?**

3 SPEAKING

PAIR WORK **Talk to your partner about the questions below. Ask for and give details.**

- What is something you said you would do this year that you have actually done?
- What is something you said you would do but haven't done?

This year I said I'd exercise more often. I've been doing my best to go to the gym at least three times a week. And I won't give up.

I said I'd give up my job and set up my own company. I've been doing a lot of research, and I'm considering different options, but I'm still working at my old job.

4 FUNCTIONAL LANGUAGE

A **Use the words and phrases below to complete the conversation.**

actually	are you sure	don't you agree
feel angry	right	that's what
think about it	what a	what you mean
would agree		

A I need to find a new apartment quickly.

B But your apartment is so nice and comfortable. [1] ______ you want to move?

A The thing is, I don't really get along with my roommate. He's so messy, [2] ______?

B Yeah, I [3] ______ with you.

A It's impossible to share a place with a person like that, [4] ______?

B I see [5] ______.

A And last week he had friends over, and there were dozens of dirty glasses on the kitchen table. [6] ______ nightmare!

B I bet that made you [7] ______.

A Angry? [8] ______, I was furious!

B Why don't you talk to him about it again? [9] ______ I'd do.

A Yeah, now that I [10] ______, he's usually a pretty good listener. I'll have a talk with him tonight.

5 SPEAKING

A PAIR WORK **Choose one of the situations below. Act it out in pairs.**

- Tell your partner about something you're thinking of buying. Your partner questions or approves of your choice. Go to page 102 for useful language.

I just saw a fantastic suitcase on sale for only $99.99.

Why would you want to buy a new suitcase? You aren't planning to travel this year.

Well, it's on sale, and …

- Discuss with your partner. Which is better: working for a big, global company or setting up your own company? Give your opinions. Try to get your partner to agree. Go to page 112 for useful language.

I think it's better to set up your own business. You can be more creative, and you'll probably make more money. You know what I mean?

That's a really good point, but you have to consider the risks …

- Talk to your partner about a good or bad experience you had on your last vacation. Your partner asks about or guesses how you felt. Go to page 122 for useful language.

It was an amazing trip, but on the last day, I overslept and missed the plane back.

I bet that made you feel horrible. And what did you do then?

I called the airline company, and they said that I would have to wait for the next flight …

B **Change roles and repeat the role play.**

GRAMMAR REFERENCE AND PRACTICE

7.1 USED TO (page 67)

used to				
You can use ***used to*** for actions that happened regularly in the past but do not happen now, and for states that were true in the past but are not true anymore.				
	Affirmative	**Negative**	**Questions**	**Short answer**
I / You / He / She / We / They	**used to buy** CDs.	**didn't use to like** pop music.	**Did** you **use to listen** to pop music? What **did** you **use to like**?	Yes, I **did**. No, I **didn't**.

A **Complete the sentences with the verbs in parentheses ( ) and the correct form of *used to*.**

1 Did you use to go to school with Terry Johnson? (go)
2 That company ______ famous all around the world. (be)
3 I ______ to the radio, but I don't have a radio now. (listen)
4 He ______ chocolate, but now he loves it. (not eat)
5 Who ______ she ______ married to? (be)
6 I ______ my friends at the local coffee shop. (meet)

7.2 COMPARISONS WITH *(NOT) AS … AS* (page 69)

Comparisons with *(not) as … as*					
We can use ***as*** … ***as*** to say that two things are the same or similar. ***not as*** … ***as*** means the first thing is less than the second thing.					
Subject	**Verb**	***as***	**Adjective**	***as***	
The new series	is isn't	***as***	**good** **funny**	***as***	the first series
Subject	**Verb**	***as***	**Adverb**	***as***	
I	train don't train	***as***	**hard** **often** **much**	***as***	my brother does.
Subject	**Verb**	***as***	**Noun**	***as***	
My old phone	had didn't have	***as***	**many ringtones** **much memory**	***as***	my new one.

A **Are the sentences true (T) or false (F)? Change one or two words in each false sentence to make it true.**

1 F Tablet screens are as big as TV screens. Tablet screens aren't as big as TV screens.
2 ___ Birds can fly as fast as planes. ______
3 ___ Movies aren't as long as series. ______
4 ___ Buses don't have as many seats as movie theaters. ______
5 ___ Shoes aren't as expensive as socks. ______
6 ___ A lake has as much water as an ocean. ______

8.1 PRESENT PERFECT CONTINUOUS (page 77)

Present perfect continuous	
Use the present perfect continuous for an action or event that started in the past and continues into the present time.	
What **have** you **been doing**? I'**ve been painting** pictures recently. I **haven't been going out** lately. What **has** she **been doing**? She'**s been making** sushi lately. She **hasn't been eating out** recently.	**Have you been going out** lately? Yes, I have. No, I haven't. **Has** he **been playing** soccer recently? Yes, he has. No, he hasn't.

A **Complete the conversation with the present perfect continuous of the verbs in parentheses ( ).**

A What [1] ___are___ you [2] ___doing___ at work these days? (do)

B I [3] ________ software. (design)

A That's interesting. [4] ________ you [5] ________ with other people? (work)

B Yes, I [6] ________ . I [7] ________ with a guy in our Japan office. (work)

A Will you have the opportunity to go to Japan?

B I think so. My boss [8] ________ a trip for me, but it won't happen this month. (plan)

A So, [9] ________ you [10] ________ any fun lately? (have)

B No, I [11] ________ ! I [12] ________ at all, but I have some free time this weekend (not go out). Let's meet up!

8.2 PRESENT PERFECT VS. PRESENT PERFECT CONTINUOUS (page 79)

Present perfect vs. present perfect continuous **Present perfect**	**Present perfect continuous**
I'**ve cleaned** the bathroom. I'**ve made** some cookies. She'**s worked** for the company for 24 years. So far, we'**ve watched** four episodes of the series. We'**ve watched** that movie twice.	I'**ve been cleaning** the bathroom. I'**ve been making** cookies. That's why the kitchen is a mess. She'**s been working** for the company for three months. I'**ve been going** to the gym three times a week.

A **Complete the sentences with the verbs in parentheses ( ). Use the present perfect or the present perfect continuous.**

1 I ___'ve been riding___ my mountain bike a lot recently. (ride)
2 My essay is going well. I ________ six pages so far. (write)
3 We just got here. We ________ for long. (not wait)
4 Sorry about my dirty clothes. I ________ on my car. (work)
5 I was born in this town. I ________ here since 1998. (live)
6 She's getting better on the guitar. She ________ every day. (practice)
7 You can't look at my painting. I ________ it. (not finish)
8 He knows how to make cookies. He ________ them before. (make)

9.1 MODALS OF NECESSITY: *HAVE TO, NEED TO, MUST* (page 87)

Modals of necessity: *have to, need to, must*	
I **have to** / **need to take** enough courses to get a degree. I **don't have to** / **don't need to choose** a job yet.	Why do you **have to** / **need to get** a degree? Do you **have to** / **need to choose** a major? Yes, I do. / No, I don't.
NOTE: We mainly use must ***in formal situations.*** Students **must enroll** in four classes each semester.	

A **Complete the sentences with the correct form of the words in parentheses ( ).**

1 He ______ call the office in San Francisco right away. (need to)
2 You ______ buy us a gift, but it was very nice of you. (not have to)
3 The college ______ reply within ten days. (must)
4 How much homework ______ you ______ do last night? (have to)
5 She ______ make a decision now. (not need to)
6 ______ we ______ have a degree to get a job at that company? (have to)

9.2 MODALS OF PROHIBITION AND PERMISSION (page 89)

Modals of prohibition and permission	
Use *can't* and *must not* + the base form of a verb to say what is prohibited or what is not allowed. *Must not* is stronger than *can't*. When speaking, we often use *can't* instead of *must not*.	
Prohibition: *can't, must not*	**Permission: *can, may, could***
You **can't waste** time. We **can't leave** work early. You **must not do** chores around the house. They **must not take** their laptops out of the building.	You **can** / **may** take short breaks. They **can** / **may** work from home on Fridays. **Can** / **Could** / **May** I email you? – Yes, you **can** / **may**. – No, you **can't** / **may not**.

A **Cross out the word or phrase that does not work in each sentence.**

1 The official company handbook says: "You ~~can~~ / *must not* / *can't* have drinks at your desk because they might spill."
2 We need to be in the office four days a week, but we *can* / *may* / *could* work from home on Fridays.
3 **A** *Can* / *Must* / *Could* I use your laptop? **B** Sure. No problem.
4 **A** May I come to work a few minutes late tomorrow? **B** Yes, you *can* / *could* / *may*.
5 Employers *can't* / *must not* / *couldn't* hire people without experience.
6 You *can* / *can't* / *may* have the meeting in my office tomorrow. There's enough room for everyone.

> **!** **We often use *please* when asking for permission.**
> *Can I **please** come to work late tomorrow?*
> *Can I come to work late tomorrow, **please**?*
> **Don't use *could* in statements. This shows a possibility, not permission.**

10.1 SIMPLE PRESENT PASSIVE (page 99)

Simple present passive

We use the passive when we're more interested in the action, or in the person or thing receiving the action – and less interested in, or don't know, the person or thing doing the action. We can use *by* to say who or what is doing the action.

The furniture **is made** in this factory. The chairs **are used** in restaurants. The price **isn't written** on the label. The beds **aren't sold** in the US. The meals **are cooked** by a famous chef.	Where **are** the beds **sold**? **Are** the beds **sold** in the US? **Yes**, they **are**. / **No**, they **aren't**.

A **Write the sentences in the passive.**

1 They make all the furniture from wood. All the furniture is made from wood.
2 You cook the dish in the oven. ______
3 They sell the snacks at local supermarkets. ______
4 Where do you find these plants? ______
5 Do they play the sport in Mexico? ______
6 You don't eat the dish in summer. ______
7 They use this technology in hospitals. ______
8 You don't see the animals during the day. ______

10.2 SIMPLE PAST PASSIVE (page 101)

Simple past passive

My laptop **was designed** in the US. This dress **was designed by** my friend. The coffee beans **were imported**. My laptop **wasn't made** in the US. The coffee beans **weren't grown** in Canada.	**Was** the fruit **picked** and **frozen** right away? Yes, it **was**. / No, it **wasn't**. **Were** the computers **shipped** from China? Yes, they **were**. / No, they **weren't**. Where **were** the computers **shipped** from? Who **were** the computers **shipped by**?

A **Circle the correct active or passive verb.**

1 I *bought / was bought* a tablet online. It *shipped / was shipped* to me right away.
2 These pictures *painted / were painted* by my sister. She *trained / was trained* really well.
3 My house *built / was built* more than 100 years ago. I have no idea who *built / was built* it.
4 These shoes *made / were made* locally, but those *imported / were imported* from Italy.
5 She *sent / was sent* the birthday card on Tuesday, and it *delivered / was delivered* the next day.
6 I *caught / was caught* this fish last summer and *froze / was frozen* it right away.

11.1 PHRASAL VERBS (page 109)

Phrasal verbs		
No object	**With object, separable**	**With object, inseparable**
Things hardly ever **work out** the first time. You need to **stand out**. Don't **give up** when it gets tough.	They **set up** a company. (They **set** it **up**.) I **figured out** the answer. (I **figured** it **out**.) **Keep up** the hard work. (**Keep** it **up**.) **Give up** candy and you'll feel better. (**Give** it **up**.)	**Get over** the problem. (**Get over** it.) **Work at** something you're good at. (**Work at** it.)

A **Complete the sentences. Put the second word of the verb and *it* in the correct order.**

1 When did you set ___it up___? up / it
2 I just can't figure ______? out / it
3 She's really working ______. at / it
4 I've decided to give ______. up / it
5 You'll get ______ soon. over / it
6 I hope you keep ______. up / it

11.2 PRESENT AND FUTURE UNREAL CONDITIONALS (page 111)

Present and future unreal conditionals	
The present and future unreal conditional describes the possible result of an imagined situation in the present or future.	
Condition (*if* clause)	**Result (main clause)**
If you **had** a million dollars,	what **would** you **do**?
If I **had** a million dollars,	I'**d start** a business.
If I **had** a million dollars,	I **wouldn't work**.
If I **offered** you a million dollars,	**would** you **swim** across a river full of crocodiles? Yes, I **would**. No, **I wouldn't**.

A **Complete the sentences with the correct form of the verbs in parentheses ( ).**

1 If Viggo ___had___ (have) a better job, he ___would be___ (be) happier.
2 Lorenzo ______ (walk) to work if he ______ (live) closer.
3 I ______ (consider) moving to Japan if I ______ (not have) a cat.
4 If we ______ (start) a business, we ______ (not see) our friends much.
5 If I ______ (be) you, I ______ (do) more research before making a decision.
6 Mara ______ (not know) what to do if her parents ______ (not help) her.

> **!**
> **'d = would wouldn't = would not**
> **The condition (*if* clause) can also be in the second part of the sentence. Note there is no comma when the result (main clause) is first.**
> *What would happen **if** I won the race?*
> *You would be famous **if** you won the race.*

12.1 INDEFINITE PRONOUNS (page 119)

Indefinite pronouns			
Indefinite pronouns are used when the noun is unknown or not important.			
with *every-*	**with *some-***	**with *any-***	**with *no-***
Everyone was mad at me.	Can **someone** pass me the ketchup?	**Anyone** can make a mistake.	**No one** / **Nobody** blamed me for the accident.
The peas flew **everywhere**.	My wallet fell out of my bag **somewhere**.	I can't find the salt **anywhere**.	There's **nowhere** to eat in this area.
I ate **everything** on my plate.	Would you like **something** to eat?	Can I help you with **anything**?	Is there really **nothing** in the fridge?

A **Circle the correct indefinite pronouns.**

> **!** *No one* is two words. The other indefinite pronouns are one word.

1 I asked *someone* / *anyone* about the café, but he didn't know *nothing* / *anything* about it.

2 The kids want to watch *anything* / *something* on TV. Is there *anything* / *everything* good on right now?

3 Let's go *anywhere* / *somewhere* nice for lunch. Does *anybody* / *nobody* know a great restaurant?

4 *No one* / *Anyone* can join the company gym, and it's free. It doesn't cost *anybody* / *anything*.

5 I've made *something* / *anything* for dinner. It's *nothing* / *something* special, but I hope you like it.

6 *Everyone* / *Anyone* loves this beach. They say there's *nowhere* / *everywhere* like it.

12.2 REPORTED SPEECH (page 121)

Reported speech		
Reported speech tells us what someone says in another person's words. In reported speech, we use a reporting verb – for example, *say* or *tell* – followed by a *that* clause.		
Tense / Verb	**What someone said (direct speech)**	**How it's reported (reported speech)**
Simple present	"I **play** baseball."	She said that she play**ed** baseball.
Present continuous	"I**'m** work**ing** all day."	He said he **was** work**ing** all day.
Simple past	"I **spoke** to Ken."	He told me that he **had spoken** to Ken.
Present perfect	"I**'ve seen** the report."	She told me she **had seen** the report.
Future with *going to*	"I**'m going to** quit my job."	He said he **was going to** quit his job.
Future with *will*	"I**'ll** call you soon."	She said that she **would** call me soon.
can	"I **can** see you on Friday."	He told me he **could** see me on Friday.

A **Write what the person said.**

1 He said that he was thrilled with the idea. "I'm thrilled with the idea."

2 She said she couldn't come to the party. "I ______."

3 He told me he was going to eat out. "I ______."

4 She told me that she wouldn't be home. "I ______."

5 He said that he was going shopping. "I ______."

VOCABULARY PRACTICE

7.1 MUSIC (page 66)

A Circle the type of music that matches the definition.

1. a type of popular music with a strong beat, often played with electric guitars and drums: *classical / rock*
2. a type of popular music from Jamaica with a strong beat: *reggae / folk*
3. modern music with a strong beat that many young people like listening and dancing to: *country / pop*
4. a form of music developed mainly in the 18th and 19th centuries: *classical / EDM*
5. music that people often play without looking at written music: *jazz / folk*
6. a style of harsh, distorted rock music played loudly on electric instruments: *reggae / heavy metal*
7. a type of pop music with a strong beat in which people often speak the words: *hip-hop / jazz*
8. music written and played in a traditional style: *rock / folk*
9. a style of popular music from the southern and western US: *country / reggae*
10. a type of dance music with a strong beat usually played at clubs and festivals: *classical / EDM*

B Cover exercise A and complete the words with the missing letters.

1. r *e g g a* e
2. c _ _ _ _ _ _ _ l
3. h _ _ _ _ m _ _ _ _
4. c _ _ _ _ _ y
5. j _ _ _
6. f _ _ _
7. h _ _ – _ _ _
8. r _ _ _

7.2 TV SHOWS AND MOVIES (page 68)

A Match the kinds of TV shows or movies with the emojis.

1. science fiction *e*
2. romantic comedy ___
3. horror ___
4. game show ___
5. musical ___
6. comedy ___

B Complete the actor's story with kinds of TV shows or movies from exercise A.

When I was 18, I was on a [1] ______________, and I won $2,000! That was my first time on TV. I really liked it, so I tried out for a small part in a TV series, and I got it. It was [2] ______________, and my character traveled through time. It was so cool! After that, I did a [3] ______________ movie. I'm not crazy about scary stuff usually, but it was better to act in it than to watch it! I think I want to try something lighter next time, though. Something fun, like a [4] ______________ where my character falls in love with a celebrity. Or maybe a regular [5] ______________, where I get all the laughs. But I don't think I'll do a [6] ______________. My singing voice isn't that great!

8.1 DESCRIBING EXPERIENCES (page 76)

A **Complete the sentences with the correct words. Then change the underlined words so the sentences are true for you.**

challenge change chore opportunity success

1 I think washing dishes is a boring ________.
2 Passing my driver's test was a difficult ________.
3 Tina's surprise birthday party was a great ________.
4 I'm ready for a ________ in my style. I want a new hairstyle.
5 I'd love to have an ________ to travel to Argentina.

B **Circle the correct words to complete the paragraph.**

I had an interesting experience at work last month. I had to work on a group [1]*project / change* with three other people. We had to design a new website for our company. It was a difficult [2]*opportunity / job*, but we thought of an interesting [3]*chore / process* – we each took one part of the design to work on and then showed each other our work. I designed the homepage. The new website was a [4]*success / challenge*, so our boss was happy. I hope to have [5]*an opportunity / a change* to work with the group in the future.

8.2 DESCRIBING PROGRESS (page 78)

A **Complete the sentences with the correct words. You will use one of the words twice.**

concentrate do have save spend take waste

1 I'm sure we'll ________ trouble with this.
2 We have plenty of extra time. We can ________ it easy.
3 I don't ________ time for a break while I'm doing this.
4 If we want to finish this, we can't ________ time.
5 We'll have to ________ our best on this.
6 I'm sure we can do this quickly and ________ a lot of time.
7 This is very complex work. We really need to ________ on this.
8 I'll have to ________ a lot of time on this.

B **Which sentences from exercise A are possible before the sentence below? Check (✓) the sentences.**

"________. It's a really difficult job."

☐ 1 ☐ 2 ☐ 3 ☐ 4
☐ 5 ☐ 6 ☐ 7 ☐ 8

9.1 COLLEGE SUBJECTS (page 86)

A Complete the sentences with the correct words. There are four extra words.

architecture	biology	business	chemistry	computer science	economics
education	engineering	law	medicine	physics	political science

1 I'm studying ________ because I want to help sick people.
2 My cousin studied ________ in college, and now he designs buildings.
3 I didn't study ________ much. I just remember it was about energy and heat and light and stuff.
4 My younger sister wants to study ________ so she can understand plants and animals better.
5 Ruby is interested in politicians and power. Her degree is in ________ .
6 I'm studying ________ because I need to know how to buy and sell products and run a company.
7 When you study ________ , you learn about the impact of money on people, companies, and countries.
8 My degree is in ________ . I'm hoping to improve the roads and bridges in my country.

B Cover exercise A and complete the words with the missing letters.

1 I have a degree in a r c h i t e c t u r e.
2 Did you study b ________ y in school?
3 My mother studied e ____ n ________ s in college.
4 I'd like to take some e ____ a ____ n courses.
5 I've never studied c ____ m ________ y.
6 My parents want me to study b ________ s.
7 I'm studying c ________ r s ________ e right now.
8 P ________ s is a fascinating subject.

9.2 EMPLOYMENT (page 88)

A Complete the sentences with the correct words. There is one extra word.

apply	employer	fire	hire	profession	salary	wage	working hours

I just finished college, and now I'm going to [1] ________ for jobs as a computer tech. It's a great [2] ________ , and there are a lot of jobs. The [3] ________ for most jobs are from 9:00 a.m. to 5:00 p.m. I hope I can find an [4] ________ who will [5] ________ someone without much experience. I'd like to earn a [6] ________ , but because it's my first job, I might need to work for a [7] ________ and get paid by the hour.

B Circle the correct answers.

1 Sarah is already saving for her *employer / retirement* even though she's only in her 20s.
2 I don't know exactly what I want to do, but I'd like to have a *career / salary* in medicine.
3 My boss says she'll *fire / hire* anyone who steals information from the company.
4 Lydia has three new *wages / contracts* to design websites for people.
5 When you're self-employed, it's important to *manage / hire* your time well.

10.1 DESCRIBING MATERIALS (page 98)

A **Circle the correct adjectives. Which sentence does not include opposites?**

1 Leather is *artificial / natural.*
2 Stone is *heavy / light.*
3 Metal is *hard / soft.*
4 Glass is *fragile / strong.*
5 Cotton is *hard / soft.*
6 Polyester is *artificial / natural.*
7 Wool is *warm / waterproof.*
8 Wood is *fragile / strong.*

B **Complete the sentences with some of the materials from exercise A.**

1 ____Wool____ is natural and very warm.
2 ________ can feel cold and is fragile.
3 ________ comes from trees.
4 ________ is hard, heavy, and sometimes stronger than stone.
5 ________ is natural and can help keep you dry but is not totally waterproof.

10.2 PRODUCTION AND DISTRIBUTION (page 100)

A **Circle the correct word to complete each sentence.**

1 What time did they *deliver / store* your package?
2 How can I *design / transport* these TVs to New York?
3 I *caught / froze* a lot of fruit and vegetables this year.
4 Do they *import / export* these cars from Japan?
5 The children *produced / picked* a lot of apples yesterday.
6 My uncle's company *manufactures / grows* furniture.

B **Cross out the word that does not work in each sentence.**

1 Yesterday, I *caught / froze / picked* some peas and beans.
2 He *delivered / shipped / stored* the package to your house yesterday.
3 Did your company *design / grow / manufacture* these shoes?
4 We *deliver / import / transport* our products to customers around the world.
5 My country *exports / grows / manufactures* a lot of vegetables.

11.1 SUCCEEDING (page 108)

A **Match the first parts of the sentences (1–9) with the second parts of the sentences (a–i).**

1 I really need to **figure** b
2 The two friends decided to **set** ___
3 It took me a long time to **get** ___
4 I was so tired, I just had to **give** ___
5 With his green hair, he really **stands** ___
6 You'll get your degree if you can **keep** ___
7 To become a good skier, you have to **work** ___
8 Unfortunately, my plan didn't **work** ___
9 While I was sick, I decided to **give** ___

a **out** as well as I hoped.
b **out** how to fix this.
c **out** in the photo.
d **up** the hard work until next summer.
e **up** before the end of the race.
f **up** the company six years ago.
g **up** coffee and drink only water and juice.
h **over** my bad exam results.
i **at** your technique.

B **Complete the text with five of the two-word verbs from exercise A. Use the correct form.**

The professor said to the class, "You'll never [1] figure out the solution to this problem. It's almost impossible!" But I decided I would be the one who did. I wanted to [2] ___ in my class. So I thought, "I'm really going to [3] ___ this – all day if necessary." But at midnight I was still no closer to finding the answer. So unfortunately, I had to [4] ___. I thought, "I hope nobody else in the class gets the answer, or I'll never [5] ___ it!"

11.2 OPPORTUNITIES AND RISKS (page 110)

A **Match the expressions (1–12) with the definitions (a–l).**

1 advantage ___
2 consider ___
3 disadvantage ___
4 effect ___
5 goal ___
6 option ___
7 purpose ___
8 research ___
9 result ___
10 reward ___
11 risk ___
12 situation ___

a something you want to do in the future
b a choice
c the possibility of something bad happening; to do something although something bad might happen
d the set of things that are happening at a particular time and place
e something that happens because something else has happened
f why you do something
g the study of a subject to get new information; to study a subject to get more information
h something good that you get because you have done something good
i to think about something carefully
j something good that helps you
k a change caused by something else
l something that makes a situation more difficult

B **Complete the paragraph with words from exercise A.**

My [1] goal is to study English in Australia for a year. I can study in Melbourne or Sydney. I'll probably take the second [2] ___. I plan to quit my job at the end of the year and go to Sydney after that. It's a [3] ___, but I think it's worth it. It'll have a big [4] ___ on my life. One [5] ___ is that my English will be excellent when I return. A [6] ___ is that I won't make much money while I'm in Australia. I might [7] ___ getting a part-time job after I get there, but I want to spend most of my time studying. The main [8] ___ of my year abroad is to study as much as I can.

12.1 DESCRIBING ACCIDENTS (page 118)

A **Circle the correct verbs to complete the sentences.**

1 She *picked up / pulled out* the broken glass from the table.
2 I dropped and broke my phone and *felt bad about / blamed* it.
3 My ring *shook / slipped* off my finger and disappeared.
4 I *spilled / knocked off* some coffee on my new white rug.
5 My brother *damaged / destroyed* his bike, but he can still ride it.
6 Did you leave the lights *open / on*?
7 When I opened the door of my car, two bags of groceries *fell out / pulled out*.
8 Don't *leave open / shake* that box. You don't know what's in it.

B **Match the first parts of the sentences (1–8) with the second parts of the sentences (a–h).**

1 He left his computer ___
2 I picked up ___
3 Someone left ___
4 I hope you aren't mad ___
5 He pulled all the things ___
6 She feels really ___
7 His hand slipped, and he knocked ___
8 I picked up the bottle and ___

a the back door open.
b bad about the accident.
c the glass onto the floor.
d on by accident.
e at Susan.
f shook it.
g out of the cupboard and cleaned it.
h my keys from the floor.

12.2 DESCRIBING EXTREMES (page 120)

A **Match the first parts of the sentences (1–10) with the second parts of the sentences (a–j).**

1 It's the most enormous TV I've ever seen. It's ___
2 I stood in the snow and waited for two hours. I was ___
3 What time are we having dinner? I'm ___
4 We had a terrific view of Rio from the plane. It was ___
5 Aren't you too hot in that big sweater? You must be ___
6 I can't read this. The writing is ___
7 She said it was the best gift she'd ever had. She was ___
8 The kids had a great vacation, but now it's over, so they're ___
9 I haven't slept for 36 hours. I'm ___
10 I'm scared of spiders. When I see one, I'm ___

a boiling.
b thrilled.
c exhausted.
d freezing.
e huge.
f magnificent.
g miserable.
h starving.
i terrified.
j tiny.

B **Complete the sentences with all possible words. Use each word once.**

boiling	enormous	exhausted	freezing	huge	magnificent
miserable	starving	terrific	terrified	thrilled	tiny

1 When I opened the box and saw what was in it, I was *terrified* / *thrilled*.
2 I don't feel good. I'm ___ / ___ / ___ / ___ / ___.
3 Look at the size of that dog! It's ___ / ___ / ___!
4 Wow, look at that view. It's ___ / ___.

PROGRESS CHECK

Can you do these things? Check (✓) what you can do. Then write your answers in your notebook.

UNIT 7

Now I can …	Prove it
☐ talk about different kinds of music.	Write down as many kinds of music as you can. Say which ones are your top three favorite kinds. Say which ones you don't like.
☐ use *used to*.	Write three sentences about things you used to do at different stages of your life but don't do now.
☐ talk about TV shows and movies.	What have you watched on TV in the past week? Say what kinds of shows / movies they were.
☐ make comparisons with (*not*) *as … as*.	Choose two movies or TV shows that are similar. Say which you prefer, and explain why one isn't as good as the other.
☐ refuse invitations and respond to refusals.	Write two ways to refuse an invitation and two ways to respond to a refusal.
☐ write a movie review.	Look at your review from lesson 7.4. Can you make it better? Find three ways.

UNIT 8

Now I can …	Prove it
☐ describe experiences.	Complete the sentence with as many nouns as possible: *Cleaning the house is a difficult* ______________ .
☐ use the present perfect continuous.	Write two things you have been doing lately. Write two things you haven't been doing.
☐ describe progress.	Write a short paragraph about how you've been spending your time lately. Say if you've been making good progress.
☐ use the present perfect and the present perfect continuous.	Think about a project you've been doing but haven't finished. Write about what you've done so far.
☐ catch up with people's news.	Write down two expressions to ask about someone's news and two expressions to answer those questions.
☐ write a post about managing my time.	Look at your post from lesson 8.4. Can you make it better? Find three ways.

UNIT 9

Now I can …	Prove it
☐ talk about college subjects.	Write down as many words for college subjects as you can.
☐ use modals of necessity.	Write down two things you have to do soon and two things you don't need to do.
☐ talk about employment.	What the difference between *salary* and *wage*? What's the difference between *apply*, *hire*, and *fire*?
☐ use modals of prohibition and permission.	Write three rules for studying at a library. Use *can*, *can't*, and *must not*.
☐ express confidence and lack of confidence.	Write a response to the statement saying how confident you are: **A** *I want you to run a marathon with me.* **B** ______________
☐ write the main part of a résumé.	Look at your résumé from lesson 9.4. Can you make it better? Find three ways.

PROGRESS CHECK

Can you do these things? Check (✓) what you can do. Then write your answers in your notebook.

UNIT 10	Now I can …	Prove it
	☐ describe materials.	What materials are the clothes you're wearing today made of? Are they warm? Waterproof? Light?
	☐ use the present simple form of the passive.	Write two sentences about things that are recycled and two sentences about things that aren't recycled.
	☐ talk about production and distribution.	Write four sentences about products in your country. Use the verbs *export*, *manufacture*, *grow*, and *design*.
	☐ use the past simple form of the passive.	Write sentences using these passive verbs and your own ideas: *was made*, *were imported*, and *was invited*.
	☐ question or approve of someone's choices.	Write two expressions you can use to question someone's choices and two expressions to approve of someone's choices.
	☐ write feedback about company products.	Look at your feedback from lesson 10.4. Can you make it better? Find three ways.

UNIT 11	Now I can …	Prove it
	☐ talk about succeeding.	Complete the sentences with the missing particles: *Don't give* ________ *. You can figure it* ________ .
	☐ use phrasal verbs.	Rewrite the sentence using *it*: Deal with your problem, and work out a solution.
	☐ talk about opportunities and risks.	Write at least four sentences about a good opportunity you had. Were there any risks? What were the advantages?
	☐ use present and future unreal conditionals.	Answer the questions: *What would you buy if someone gave you $1,000? If you were a famous person, who would you be?*
	☐ give opinions and ask for agreement.	Write three things you can say when you want someone to agree with you and three things you can say to agree with someone.
	☐ write a personal story.	Look at your story from lesson 11.4. Can you make it better? Find three ways.

UNIT 12	Now I can …	Prove it
	☐ describe accidents.	Write sentences using these expressions: *damage, be mad at, knock off, feel bad about.*
	☐ use indefinite pronouns.	Write one sentence each using these words: *everyone, somewhere, anything, no one.*
	☐ describe extremes.	Write the extreme adjectives that mean the same as these phrases: *very big, very cold, very good, very hot, very sad, very tired.*
	☐ use reported speech.	Change these sentences to reported speech, beginning with *Karen said that*: "Tom left for Miami on Sunday." "Rita will finish her report soon."
	☐ describe and ask about feelings.	Write two ways to describe your feelings about a good situation and two ways to ask about someone's feelings.
	☐ write an anecdote about a life lesson.	Look at your anecdote from lesson 12.4. Can you make it better? Find three ways.

PAIR WORK PRACTICE (STUDENT A)

7.3 EXERCISE 2E STUDENT A (page 71)

1 **Invite your partner to one of the events below. Your partner refuses the invitation. Respond to your partner's refusal.**

a classical music concert | a horror movie | a baseball game

2 **Your partner invites you to an event. Refuse the invitation. Then give one of the reasons below.**

I don't really like that kind of music. I think it's sort of …

I think those movies are kind of …

I think that sport is sort of …

8.3 EXERCISE 2D STUDENT A (page 81)

1 **Imagine you are in these situations. Tell Student B about them. Listen to the reaction.**

1 I've been thinking about not eating meat anymore.
2 My brother wants a pet. He says he might get a snake.
3 How about coming with me to see the new James Bond movie?

2 **Student B will tell you some things. Make comments after each one using *That would be* and an adjective. Use the words below or your own ideas.**

amusing | difficult | nice | silly | strange | surprising | wonderful

9.3 EXERCISE 2D STUDENT A (page 91)

Ask your partner a question. Your partner says "No" and gives a reason. Then your partner asks you a question. You say "No" and give a reason using *The thing is*. Take turns.

1 Could you drive me to the airport?
2 Could you take care of my dog while I'm on vacation?
3 I'm going to paint my apartment. Can you help me?

12.3 EXERCISE 2D STUDENT A (page 123)

1 **Look at the picture. Imagine this happened to you. Tell your partner about the experience. Answer your partner's questions. Use *In the end* or *After all that* to end your story.**

2 **Listen to Student B's story. Ask questions about how your partner felt.**

PAIR WORK PRACTICE (STUDENT B)

7.3 EXERCISE 2E STUDENT B (page 71)

1 **Your partner invites you to an event. Refuse the invitation. Then give one of the reasons below.**

I don't really like that kind of music. I think it's sort of ...

I think those movies are kind of ...

I think that sport is sort of ...

2 **Invite your partner to one of the events below. Your partner refuses the invitation. Respond to your partner's refusal.**

a country music concert | a romantic comedy | a basketball game

8.3 EXERCISE 2D STUDENT B (page 81)

1 **Student A will tell you some things. Make comments after each one using *That would be* and an adjective. Use the words below or your own ideas.**

awful | boring | fantastic | great | impossible | interesting | surprising

2 **Imagine you are in these situations. Tell Student A about them. Listen to the reaction.**

1 Let's hide your brother's car keys and see what he does.

2 I've decided to get up early every morning and go for a run. Come with me.

3 It's our teacher's birthday tomorrow. We could give her some flowers.

9.3 EXERCISE 2D STUDENT B (page 91)

Your partner asks you a question. You say "No" and give a reason using *The thing is*. Then ask your partner a question. Your partner says "No" and gives a reason. Take turns.

1 Can we have a meeting after the lunch break?

2 I have a surfboard that I never use. Do you want it?

3 Why don't we have a barbecue this weekend?

12.3 EXERCISE 2D STUDENT B (page 123)

1 **Listen to Student A's story. Ask questions about how your partner felt.**

2 **Look at the picture. Imagine this happened to you. Tell your partner about the experience. Answer your partner's questions. Use *In the end* or *After all that* to end your story.**

This page is intentionally left blank

This page is intentionally left blank